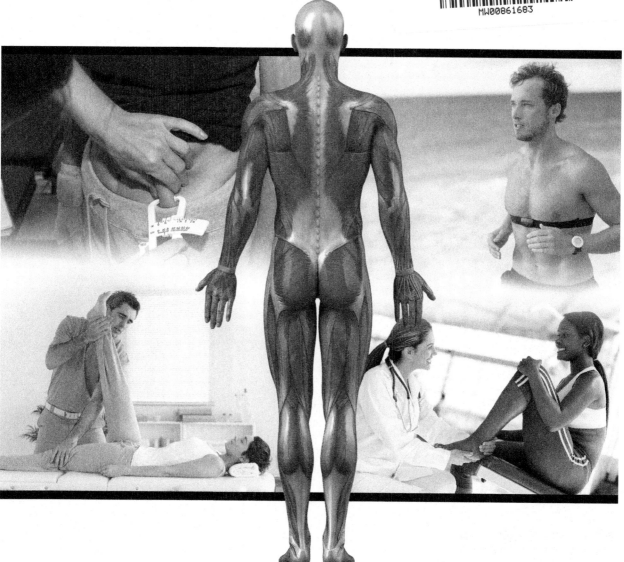

EXPLORING THE FIELD OF
KINESIOLOGY

Andrew L. Shim, Ed.D.

Kendall Hunt
publishing company

Cover image © Shutterstock, Inc.

www.kendallhunt.com
Send all inquiries to:
4050 Westmark Drive
Dubuque, IA 52004-1840

Copyright © 2015 by Kendall Hunt Publishing Company

ISBN 9781465265142

Printed in the United States of America

CONTENTS

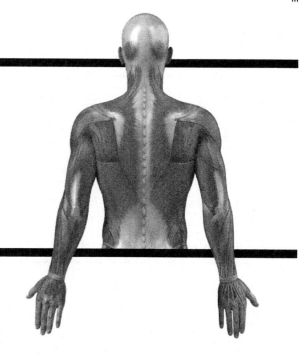

Chapter 4: Beginning Your Path in Kinesiology   33

Chapter 5: Clinical Professions   45

Chapter 6: Coaching Professions in Sport or Sport Instruction   65

Chapter 7: Teaching Careers   81

FOREWORD

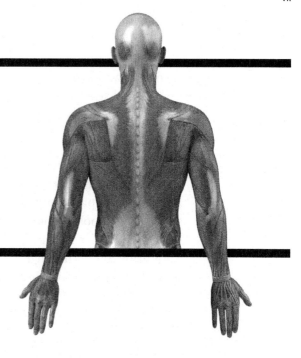

Wayne L. Westcott – Quincy College

Although I did not know it at the time, my strength training workshop at Southwestern College so many years ago was one of the most important experiences in my professional career. That was the day I first met Andrew Shim, the Department Chair of Health and Exercise Science, who graciously hosted my presentations. My trip from Boston to Chula Vista marked the beginning of a long friendship with one of the most remarkable persons I have ever known. Dr. Shim is an amazing change agent, who has had a profound positive influence in the fields of health, physical education, exercise science, kinesiology, and sports science, and has raised the bar for students and professors at all of the colleges and universities where he has taught and directed departments. For example, as Chair of the Division of Kinesiology and Sport Science at the University of South Dakota, Dr. Shim increased the program enrollment from 40 students to more than 300 students within just two years. In addition to his academic and administrative achievements, Dr. Shim has distinguished himself as a researcher, author, and speaker, as well as the editor in chief of scientific and educational journals, and the state director of major professional organizations.

Even with this brief account of Dr. Shim's breadth and depth of experiences in the aforementioned areas, it is evident that this leading professional has the education and expertise to write a comprehensive and practical textbook on kinesiology. Reading this book is essentially like having a proficient mentor take you through progressive steps to understand and appreciate this fascinating field, and to help you become fully functional in one or more of the career paths under the kinesiology umbrella.

This is a book that makes you think about important aspects of your professional life at a time when informed decisions can have incredible impact on your career success and satisfaction Dr. Shim provides highly relevant recommendations for starting your path in kinesiology, setting your goals, developing your personal management skills, and selecting your specialization, such as teaching, coaching, sports management, corporate wellness, athletic training, clinical exercise physiology, or related career tracks.

This book offers practical information on a variety of pertinent topics, including systematically navigating the many currents of undergraduate education, establishing positive and productive relationships with professors, and evaluating the efficacy of graduate school. Dr. Shim understands that life proceeds rapidly and often unexpectedly in ways for which we may be unprepared. He has, therefore, included a chapter on maintaining challenge, accomplishment, and enthusiasm throughout your career as a kinesiologist who finds meaning in what you do on a daily basis.

I cannot think of a better resource than Dr. Shim's *Exploring the Field of Kinesiology* for making an informed decision regarding a professional career in this fascinating field, and for attaining the knowledge, skills, experience, and expertise to be an influential kinesiologist who has a positive impact on peoples' lives.

CHAPTER 1
Introduction to the Field of Kinesiology

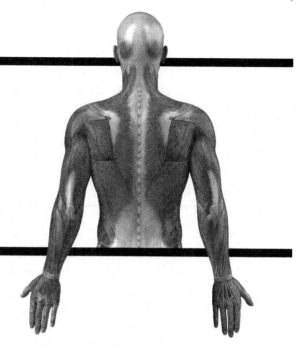

Finally, a textbook that is going to give me all the answers I actually need to obtain a promising career in the field of kinesiology. The hope remains that the first statement is true and this textbook will assist in determining your goals of selecting the right specialization or field of study. Before this journey begins, the definition of kinesiology should be discussed.

What does the term *kinesiology* mean, or represent? The word originated by the Greeks thousands of years ago to identify human movement. Kinesiology represented the study of human movement and now encompasses several umbrellas of subspecialties and career directions (Figure 1.1). Thirty years ago, this term was not available to describe the types of careers that are available today. If you were going to study human movement, you would be majoring in health or physical education. This major is still readily available at many colleges and universities nationwide, but at many institutions, it only represents pursuing a K-12 teaching profession. Today, there are misconceptions about this major such as it is only for college athletes or that it requires little preparation and involves exercising during class sessions, so it's not really an academic major. All of these are totally untrue. Many kinesiology majors go on to medical or clinical professions which require a great deal of preparation and study time. As a former kinesiology undergraduate student, I was asked about my major only to be ridiculed by my peers about the essence of playing games or sports for a grade. With regard to seeking a career, fitness or health clubs were considered the only career opportunities in the eyes of many decades past. However, this field has opened up several avenues for obtaining good paying jobs that provide upward mobility. This chapter will provide an insight to take the first step toward selecting a career under the umbrella of kinesiology. Once you have committed yourself to this, the real journey begins toward testing the waters of the subspecialties. It is expected that you will change our subspecialties along your educational path and this is considered a normal response due to your own value system changing as you mature emotionally and physically. Life events will also dictate taking different paths that were not originally considered, but makes more sense toward your own self-discovery of what defines you. So, let's take the first step and figure out who you currently are and what it will take to find your eventual career path.

Step 1: How Do I Begin?

The first step is to determine if promoting a healthy lifestyle is an integral part of your life. If so, is human movement something that interests you in some particular way? You don't have to be an athlete or be a member of a sports team to select a career in the field of kinesiology. Yes, there will be athletes (high school or college) who are connected to subspecialties of this field, which will be discussed in upcoming chapters; however, this is not considered a prerequisite toward selecting this career path. Having a passion toward understanding human movement and promoting a healthy lifestyle would be prerequisites.

Now, let's evaluate who you are. What kind of person are you? This next step is helpful toward selecting the type of human movement specialty that fits your personality and goals, based on Figure 1.2.

Figure 1.1: Directional Pattern of Kinesiology Professions

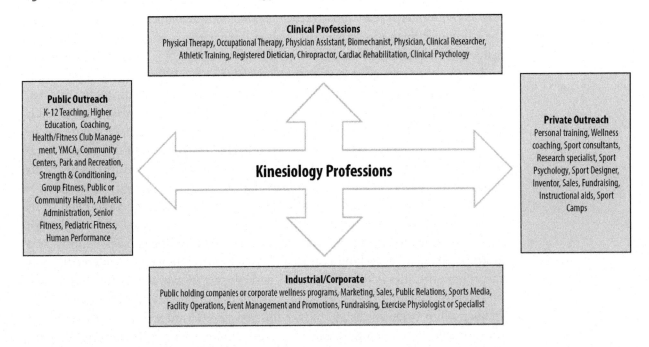

Figure 1.2: Self-Identity Path

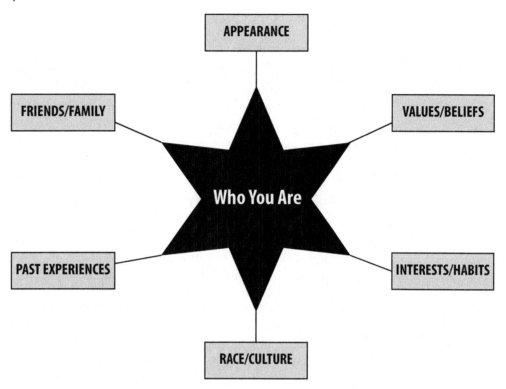

Physical appearance is usually at the top of the tier. We live in a very impressionable society and if we are going to become leaders, we must be able to demonstrate our trade skills. The field of kinesiology is led by people who tend to exhibit this in a physical manner. Not all kinesiology professions will place a major emphasis on this area, but most do. Physical fitness leaders must be able to convince their clients or patients of their knowledge base by "doing." It is much easier to provide training to others if you are able to demonstrate it works through your own lifestyle. Practicing what one preaches makes it easier to teach others about the benefits of a healthy lifestyle. Several years ago, I was at a professional personal training convention in Las Vegas, Nevada, to hear the great Jack LaLanne, the father of American fitness, receive one of the highest honors given to any fitness professional. During his acceptance speech for receiving a Lifetime Achievement Award, he quickly pointed his finger to a young personal trainer who was seated in the audience. He requested that the spotlight be placed on the young man who he pointed out and asked him to stand up. As he stood up, Jack proceeded to berate the young man for selecting the fitness profession and not looking the part. At that time, Mr. LaLanne was 75 years old and obviously was very fit. This painful lesson taught to this young man reminded me of the importance of why all kinesiology majors should maintain an appearance to demonstrate this important component of identifying who you are and what you want to represent.

Your friends and family play an important role toward developing who you are and what you want to be, especially at a young age. If you can think back upon some of your friends and families, members of this unit select careers based on what their father or mother did for a living. I have seen sons or daughters become coaches based on a parent being a successful athletic coach. This bond is very strong and tends to make a positive influence upon other family members when there is an experienced form of success. Peer pressure is another influencer when selecting a particular career that has commonality among friends or teachers who spend many hours together. A physical education teacher made an impression upon me in the fifth grade during a simple lecture about how to be a "hustler." I am sure these days that terminology will develop different responses, but back in the 1970s that expression was all about the concept of physical effort. This pep talk allowed me to ask more questions about the role of fitness and wondering if I could someday be a PE teacher like this person. I ended up becoming a PE teacher at a private charter school years later even though this became a short-term outcome. Change becomes constant as you allow other influences to affect your career decisions in the future.

Values and beliefs are important in determining who you are. This plays another important role on why this field of study is considered. Do you place an emphasis on an active or healthy lifestyle? Do you enjoy helping people become better at improving functionality or overall wellness? Does your own fitness or sport background give you essence toward this desired field? If you intend on becoming a wealthy person through this discipline, it is most likely that kinesiology is not the career path for you. The concept of "lifestyle" is a strong indicator that this value is important to promote through some form of a career. Using this component becomes desirous for many students, which propels the choice to select this type of path. Understanding how strong this can be toward selecting a career is similar to having a "calling."

Interests and/or habit are similar to beliefs and values except one can have a strong sense of urgency that wellness can improve one's overall quality of life. It doesn't always guarantee that you will practice or have an interest in pursuing this activity. Interests are based on a person's form of curiosity regarding future expectations of a behavior. In this case, it could be fitness, activity based, or sport related. Could certain interests and/or habits create a sense of value or belief over time? Perhaps, but the main point is that they are different and could lead you through the same path once you start on this journey.

Your history or past experiences play a role in selecting who you are and what you want to become. I have heard countless stories of young athletes who suffered a major injury and had to go through painful rehabilitation either by an athletic trainer or a physical therapist. This experience caused them to reflect about if this could be a future career path, working on athletes and restoring them to competitive levels. Others find a positive connection with a favorite athletic team or being at a particular place which brings a form of joy or comfort within a profession. Connecting with a professor during your college years could lead to being mentored as I was at an early stage of my academics. A simple conversation or phrase could stay with you as it did with me. A professor in my undergraduate studies asked if I wanted to be mentored by him in sport sociology and someday be a sport sociologist and teach at a university. At that time, it was a fascinating field of study but not strong enough for me to pursue this subdiscipline. Yet, it was nice to hear that I could someday be a college professor and his words have stayed with me throughout my graduate studies, ultimately leading to the teaching field in higher education.

Your race and culture complete the factors which affect your self-identity. Are you male or female? Are you Caucasian or considered a minority? Do you come from a military family or strict upbringing? Was partaking in some form of physical activity or sport considered wholesome and encouraged by your family? Are their active role models for you in the field you can relate to, based on your own background? If not, are you willing to become the role model for others to follow? Do jobs in the selected field support your ethnicity and culture? If so, must you relocate or are you able to have a sense of belonging that will allow you to become successful? I remember a few years ago, I was interviewing an African American sport management candidate for a kinesiology position in higher education. His immediate concern was the lack of fellow minority students and faculty at the institution. He turned down the position even though he was excited about the program and the opportunities it could have provided for future growth. When I was given an opportunity to begin my teaching career at an inner-city college, I gladly accepted the position even though the students were academically challenged and the crime rate was extremely high within the neighborhood. Later, I discovered the position was originally offered to a woman who quickly turned it down, based on her personal discomfort of the environment. Making deliberate decisions do affect outcomes of a career. As it later turned out, I stayed there for seven years and met wonderful people and nurturing students who I still keep in contact today. Would you work in a crime-ridden neighborhood if given opportunities to enhance your experience and career? Does your race or culture play a role with decision making within your career? Your self-identity plays an important role when given these opportunities.

Step 2: Finding the Right Program

After much reflective thought regarding who you are and what you represent, if the field of kinesiology is still considered a strong possibility, you should decide where you want to receive your educational training. There are many methods to this madness. As of late, there are over 870 fitness-related programs in this country. Where should you start to look if you already haven't done so? Before the search begins, perhaps using the following spreadsheet might be considered helpful.

Table 1.1: Selection Process for Kinesiology Programs

Name of institution	Tuition costs annually	Demographics (urban or rural)	Private or public institution	Kinesi-ology specialty	Department sponsorship or accreditation based on select-ed specialty	Faculty background in your selected area	Opportunities for students

Institution(s)

There are over 870 kinesiology programs across the United States, more so among urban-setting states such as California, Texas, and New York. Only one program exists in the State of Alaska. Of these institutions, they range in size, cost, and amenities. The best and easiest way of searching for these schools is using a search engine on the Internet. This becomes the fastest and most efficient way of navigating and comparing schools among each other. Unless distance becomes a major factor (staying closer to home within several hours of driving), this process could take several hours. The easiest method would be selecting a certain state first and finding schools in that state that have a kinesiology program. Use Table 1.1 to plot your school names first. Make additional copies of this table if needed to help you with your comparisons.

Annual Tuition Costs

For many students, the cost of education relies heavily on you and not always on your parents or guardians. This plays a major factor toward selecting a kinesiology program, especially if you are going out of state and there are no reciprocity agreements with the state of residence. Some neighboring states such as Minnesota and North Dakota allow residents to pay the same rate. Once you are able to establish residency within a calendar year, these costs will come down.

Demographics

Does the hustle and bustle of a congested major city entice you or do you prefer the quiet and calm of a smaller rural community? If so, this will also allow you to make a decision about selecting the right institution to study kinesiology. Does crime and pollution deter you from the elements of succeeding in higher education? Some students enjoy the comforts of living in a large city and having more choices of entertainment and food venues. It can make or break a selection choice based on the population as a whole. Class sizes and the ratio to student to professor are important elements to consider.

Private or Public Institution

It is a fact that public institutions are lower in tuition and fees compared to a private or faith-based institution. Does the historical, spiritual, or philosophical background of a college seem important to you? Do your beliefs create a sense of belonging toward a particular place? These are also questions you need to ask yourself as you go through your search for appropriate programs.

Kinesiology Specialty

Figure 1.1 goes over several areas of occupations within the specialties of kinesiology. For many of you, this task is difficult since there could be a variety of interests. As a former student of this exciting field, I was in the same situation. Therefore, look for kinesiology programs that offer several options to cross over or change directions without sacrificing earned credit hours while still making positive progress toward your kinesiology degree. There are many good programs nationwide that allow this to occur. Also, there will be several universities or colleges that will allow dual majors, minors, or specializations without taking extra credits beyond graduation. If you aren't sure, you will want to inquire with the department spokesperson to clarify if this can happen. As you select your specialty, there will be a time when you will be given a choice of finding an academic advisor to guide you through this finite field. To eliminate the shuffle effect of having to change advisors if you decide to change your area of interest through your academic career, you might want to seek out someone you feel could advise you in all areas, if possible. During my undergraduate studies, I changed my directions several times in the kinesiology field but found an advisor who was willing and able to work with my new interests, which worked out well in the end. Not all institutions will be flexible so you might want to keep this in mind when selecting kinesiology programs at certain universities or colleges.

Accreditation or Endorsements

This term, accreditation, usually means that a sanctioned body or major organization has granted permission to endorse or certify that this program has met certain standards or rigor to be granted privileges as being a place where students will greatly benefit in a particular field. The university or college must be accredited by certain governing bodies in order to offer legitimate degrees. You will usually find this cited on the fine print of advertisements or on the institution's webpage. However, there will be programs that do not follow or maintain certain standards to qualify for a certification or endorsement from a major organization within the kinesiology field. This does not always mean the program is not a legitimate one or lacks standards. Costs are a major factor on why a program might not have certain certifications, or the length of time a program has been in existence also plays a role in determining status. You should ask regardless, especially if you are seeking a licensure such as teaching K-12 physical education or health. As we progress throughout the chapters, we will further discuss the major organizations that are responsible for certifying or endorsing certain kinesiology specialties. This could impact where you decide to attend or learn your skills.

Faculty Background

Would you want to learn how to repair automobiles for a career from a person who has a background in furniture repair? This objective is very important along with the other categories we have covered so far, since many students just assume that your professor or lecturer is an expert in the subject area or specialty of your choice. This might not always be the case so it's best to check before selecting the right program for you. Look for faculty members who have their degrees within the field even though you might not be able to determine this right away. Also, see if the faculty webpage or directory will state their research interests, current to past publications demonstrating their expertise, and presentations they have performed over the past several years.

Are they mentoring other students in similar areas of study you are interested in? Speaking with other students who have taken them in previous classes or who have been advised by these faculty members allow you to make well-researched selections that many students are not aware of. Do they take a keen interest in student success and are they approachable? Do they make time for students even on busy days? It is expected that all faculty members who teach classes are well versed in these areas. Unfortunately, this is not the case at all institutions so it's best to check on your own before deciding on a particular program.

Opportunities for Students

Usually, this category is not advertised on a webpage but once in a while you might see this and not fully understand the importance of kinesiology departments allowing students to partake in extracurricular events to strengthen their background toward receiving a job offer when they are completed with their studies. When I was an incoming kinesiology major, I had no idea about this concept until several years later. I was fortunate I found a school that offered these opportunities that I was not aware of. Such offerings are earning internal scholarships or grants for students, joining a kinesiology club to build leadership skills, partaking in research assistant roles under a professor, becoming a selected student mentor for entry-level kinesiology students, volunteering for additional laboratory experiments, performing an undergraduate research project, assisting with departmental activities, requesting to attend professional conferences or seminars for networking possibilities that are local or regional, becoming a student ambassador for the university and supporting the kinesiology program in this manner, or becoming a member of student government and representing the department or student club in this fashion. Ask other students who have been involved and see who are the "movers and shakers" of the department. Connect with these students and find out who are the faculty members who seek out students who are willing and able to step up and get additional attention that is not required for the degree. There are many opportunities for students, if you ask the right sources and find out what is available. Eventually, most kinesiology programs will require an internship or co-op experience, which will be discussed further in another chapter. By doing your homework through building acquired skills, you become more valuable than other competitors and thus obtain greater career success than just pursuing a college degree in this field.

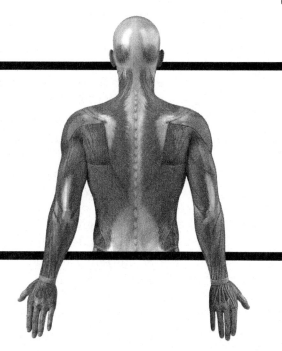

CHAPTER 2

What Is a Mentor and Why Do I Need One?

The term *mentor* was first used as a character in Homer's original poem, *The Odyssey*. When Odysseus, the king of Ithaca, decided to join forces to battle the Trojans over the beautiful Helen of Troy, he enlisted the trust of his family and his kingdom to a person named Mentor. Mentor served as the teacher and overseer of Odysseus' son, Telemachus, who grew up to avenge his family's plight—and the rest is history. Mentoring has roots where certain relationships existed in order to pass on the torch of knowledge. This knowledge or storytelling used to stay within families or organizations and now is considered a form of communication that is embraced within our society. It could be like having a big brother or big sister in certain social or business circles or having a godfather figure as a sturdy, all-knowing wise one who looked after your betterment until you earned your wings. A mentor can become a protective mechanism which could be helpful as you work your way up the knowledge ladder in the kinesiology field. So, do you feel having a mentor or mentors is a necessity toward promoting career success? There are no rules about mentoring or the number of mentors one could have. It's about a form of mutual respect and possibly having mentors who are in different areas of this major that could become advantageous, which will be discussed further in the chapter.

Characteristics of a Good Mentor

What are common characteristics of a good mentor in the field of kinesiology? First of all, we have to separate the concept of parenting from mentoring. Sure, there could be some similarities between the two concepts; however, they are also completely different. Raising someone to be a good citizen and a productive person within society is important as a role of parenting. It doesn't mean you won't have the preparation skills to become successful from good parenting. Most parents won't have the background in kinesiology to assist you with your eventual career opportunities. Therefore, seeking others to provide this insight becomes important when you become exposed to this exciting field. Finding the right people for guidance is invaluable and helps decrease the potholes of disappointments I have seen in classmates who did not find or connect with a mentor in this major. Let's go over some common characteristics to help you improve the chances of connecting with the right people in the industry.

1. Willingness to be a mentor
2. Is considered a role model
3. Investment in the field
4. Passion for the field
5. Demonstrates growth
6. Feedback of others in the field
7. Respected in the field
8. Continues to set goals
9. Values opinions of others
10. Considered as a motivator

Table 2.1: Qualifying a Mentor in the Field of Kinesiology

Characteristics	Yes	No	Not Sure
Willingness to become a mentor			
Role model in kinesiology			
Are they invested in the field?			
Demonstrates passion for the field			
Demonstrates growth in the field			
Positive feedback from people in the industry			
Well respected in the field			
Continues to set goals			
Values the opinions of others			
Is a motivator for others			

Willingness to Be a Mentor

It takes more than shaking the hand of a person who you feel is fully qualified to be a mentor. Willingness is more than just a verbal "yes, I will be your mentor" reply. There are instances when an agreement is done informally, not truly knowing that you have found a mentor. In high school, students connect with teachers or coaches who have influenced the student in a positive manner. A friendship is formed during this time and continues for several years without any confirmation of a mentorship taking place. However, this teacher or coach has become a mentor by the amount of time spent providing information that has been helpful toward making future decisions with career issues. There are instances when students develop a mentee–mentor relationship with their academic advisor in college. I have had several mentors in different capacities of my career. My academic advisor was one of my professors I met while taking her course during my freshman year. I was fortunate that I was allowed to switch advisors due to vacancies she had based on graduations. I enjoyed her class and thought she would advise me in a similar manner, a nurturing style I preferred over an authoritarian method used by my original advisor. I was never in a position to ask her to be my mentor since I was never exposed to such a concept. However, once academic advising took place, conversations would ensue about my career and my strengths on how the field of kinesiology would work for me. I was not interested in pursuing her area of study even though I enjoyed the course. Still, she would encourage me to improve my GPA, get involved with student clubs, and obtain leadership roles among the student body. She was very instrumental toward opening up several doors for me in regard to scholarships, becoming a professional reference for my part-time employment opportunities, and sponsoring me toward applying for graduate school. When she finally retired, I was the first advisee to volunteer to present her with a recognition award, on behalf of all the students she touched in a personal way. Never once did I ask for her to be a mentor to me but she was a good mentor. To this day, I keep this picture of both of us as a reminder of how strong mentorship can be toward promoting career success, especially in this discipline.

Is Considered a Role Model

When you think of the term "role model" in the field of kinesiology, what person comes to mind? If not the name of a person, how would you describe such an individual?

Remembering Jack LaLanne

Reprinted by permission of www.jacklalanne.com.

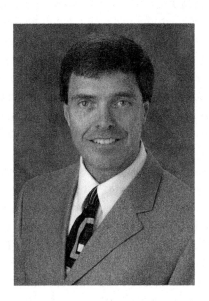

Meet Wayne Westcott
One of the most respected and celebrated individuals in the entire health industry.

When Dr. Westcott and Gary teamed up in 1998 to conduct a research project at a nursing home in Orange County, Florida, they validated the clinical and financial viability of a program format (created by Reinl – 1994 and enhanced by Westcott/Reinl – 1999) that has been integrated into more than 450 senior living facilities. Their most recent collaboration, Get Stronger, Feel Younger, is a seamless combination of their talents. The "program" effortlessly merges Dr. Westcott's vast knowledge of the field of exercise with Reinl's well-honed communication and program development skills.

Reprinted by permission of Wayne Westcott.

As your knowledge progresses within the discipline of kinesiology, so will your overall ideas of who you believe is a role model, especially to you. This is based on gaining more understanding about this field and learning about the people who have created positive changes. In my youth, I was mesmerized with the physical accomplishments of Jack LaLanne. He demonstrated that fitness was a lifetime commitment and no one had any excuse not to partake in physical activity. I also felt a connection with Bruce Jenner, the 1976 Gold Medal winner in the decathlon. I got goose bumps watching him cross the finish line after running the last event of the decathlon, waving the American flag while the TV announcers called him the greatest athlete on the planet. Seeing him on every box of Wheaties at the grocery store made me feel that I wanted to be like him, a fit person who is recognized for doing something positive in life. At an early age, these were my impressionable role models. As I started my academic training, I learned about certain researchers who were making great strides in controversial areas of fitness, senior fitness. One of these men was Dr. Wayne Westcott. Dr. Westcott was a name I recognized through my undergraduate studies and into my graduate work, especially in the area of strength and conditioning. After several chance meetings, I was finally able to spend some quality time getting to know the person when he was hired to provide curriculum training for my staff years ago when the decision was made to use his research for our fitness lab students. His enthusiasm and endless energy was infectious while we spent countless hours discussing the field of kinesiology and the direction it was headed. The conversation also developed toward my own professional development and the need to refine my research skills. Never once did I formally ask him to be my mentor but he became an important one for me through his willingness to guide me through the world of research and academia. His accomplishments—author of over 24 books, endless publications, nationally sought-after speaker, and the owner of two lifetime achievement awards, and taking the time to maintain his high fitness levels—make him an absolute role model in this field. I am grateful to this day to call him my role model, mentor, and good friend.

Investment in the Field

When discussing the term *investment*, there are several scenarios that appear to make sense. As a banker would note, do you place your money or items of value in a specific area where it will increase in value? I would analogize this to identifying if a potential mentor has accomplished this task. If you look back at the historical start of a possible candidate, has this person become "vested" in the discipline? Are such persons involved in a specific area of study and have they stayed in the area that you are thinking about pursuing? Are they able to discuss the climate of how their expertise in a subdivision has developed and how they responded to changes within the industry to make the modifications to stay connected in the field? Do you still see continued accomplishments that would demonstrate that this person is fully vested and continues to increase the stock of knowledge in our field? These are clear signs of the metaphors, "Practice what you preach" and "Say as I do." The credibility is obvious and continues as time moves forward. This is another positive characteristic of a possible mentor that would be considered as a proper selection. A penny stock should be worth over a dollar within a period of time if wisely invested by your mentor.

Passion for the Field

Endless energy, eyes widened, and the tone of voice sounding ecstatic when discussing current projects or opportunities but without distractions—these are characteristics of persons who are passionate for their field of study. Shouldn't everyone be this way? Apparently this isn't always the case so it's important to figure out if you also share this vision and energy for a particular field in kinesiology. When I am discussing what I do for a profession or the types of projects I am personally involved with, common comments I receive back from strangers to parents is, "I can tell you are passionate about your job." Why shouldn't it always be that way? It is if you find the right people to mentor you who also share this feeling of excitement about this profession. I tell others that the moment I don't have the fire or drive anymore, it would be time to find another profession. Having the zest to come to work every day and enjoy what you do and the people who work with you or from you plays a role that ensures altruism. Altruism is a very strong concept, allowing people to improve their self-esteem and worth by giving back to others without reciprocity. Altruism also promotes passion since you are giving your time, energy, and effort to a cause that you feel extremely strongly about. When I advise kinesiology majors for the first time and many of these students are unaware of what they really want to do for a career, I sometimes ask, "What is something you would basically do for free and continue to do this, even though there were no promises of a future payment?" This becomes a true act of passion and having a mentor express and demonstrate this concept is an important characteristic to possess.

Demonstrates Growth

Investment and growth have commonalities to each other. Being in the industry for many years and being known is one thing, showing the adaptation of growth is another. Here is a good example of the lack of growth but having the investment of being in the field. I attended a national convention a few years back and decided to hear a well-known researcher speak about a kinesiology topic. It was very disappointing to me when his PowerPoint presentation had not been updated for at least 10 years, based on the dates of his references. The presentation lacked recent changes in the industry and was a rehash of what this researcher has done up until the last 10 years. For a person of his stature, I felt he has lost his ability to keep up with the changes that have taken place, especially in the area of technology. Technology is a tricky term to use since most people associate the word with electronic items or concepts of utilizing information in a quicker manner. Have I met professors who do not use email or their answering machines? The answer is yes because they choose not to grow with the modern times of information dissemination. Others will choose not to stay involved with the changes that take place in their field of study. It's tough to do so but this is the way our industry survives. This form of Darwinism exists in all facets of life. There was a phase a biology professor told me during grad school, that if we aren't willing to change, biologically you will cease to exist. Former mammal species either had to make adaptations based on the change of their environment or they would cease to exist. Growth also means adaptation within this field and a true mentor should also exhibit these adaptations besides being well invested.

Feedback from Others in the Field

Look for mentors who are being recognized for their efforts in the field of kinesiology by their peers, whether this be local, regionally, and nationally. This is another major sign that this person is being productive and is still connected to the profession. Service awards are a sign of receiving feedback. Your peers are appreciative of the work and/or changes that this person has contributed to. Longevity does not always guarantee a service or lifetime achievement award. One does not have to advertise to let others know what has been accomplished or completed. Your work eventually does gain a reputation within the industry and people do recognize this over a period of time. Many years ago, another mentor of mine named Bill Tom was being honored as a recipient into the Gymnastics Hall of Fame in Lincoln, Nebraska. Bill was a former Olympic gymnast for the United States in 1956 and still the oldest male ever to make the U.S. gymnastics squad at age 33. At the age of 73, he was finally inducted into this prestigious group of world-class athletes. At a press conference, he was asked how one gets into the Hall of Fame? He paused for several seconds and then replied, "if you live long enough, you will get there." It made us laugh at the time he said this, but I disagreed with his statement years later. It is your accomplishments and being recognized by your peers that got you in. Someone finally recognized that at age 33, it's very difficult to make any Olympic team, especially in the sport of gymnastics. He never won an Olympic medal during the 1956 games held in Melbourne, Australia; however, his contributions toward the sport after he retired also played an important role for his entry into the Hall. If one continues to do good things in the field, the right people do remember these good things eventually. Your commitment plays a key role and a good mentor will assist with promoting this characteristic by actions and not by words.

Respected in the Field

"Respect yourself and others will respect you." —Confucius, *Sayings of Confucius*

How do we determine if someone is well respected in this field? Is it based on personality, good looks, charm, or overall contributions to the discipline of kinesiology? If you look at several definitions of the term *respect*, most will agree among your peers of a certain level of worth that is placed upon that individual. It may be based on several factors we have already described as a good mentor. Is this person held in high esteem among peers in the field? As the earlier quotation from Confucius, you cannot demand respect from others. Through hard work and determination, this concept will be attained since it is earned and not given. The mentors I have personally had over several decades in this field have been people who were doers. My good friend Bill Tom kept competing in several Senior Olympic events, winning titles in badminton, swimming, table tennis, diving, and tennis until his death at age 89. He told me a year before he passed away, his doctors asked that he stop competing in sports since he could die from the physical competition. He said he would rather die on the badminton courts than in a hospital. He had a rough upbringing when he was young since his parents didn't have money for him to go to school. When he had the opportunity to give to people in need, he was always the first to lend a hand. I didn't always agree on his pedagogy techniques on how he taught certain classes but I learned to realize that everyone has their strengths and weaknesses. He showed me that respect doesn't always come all at once, it comes in handfuls at certain times and hearing it from verbal comments is not how respect is given. It's also received in the form of actions from individuals, years later who come to realize the lessons that were taught were finally learned.

Continues to Set Goals

Being challenged is a part of living. Without this, why would you want to continue to pursue your dreams if it was so easy to obtain? You would not respect the process or your accomplishments. When I began teaching a Taekwondo course at a local community college years ago, a beginning student approached me during my office hours and asked a question. He asked why I stopped competing in tournaments. I said after many years of regional and national competitions, most people my age retire from competition and teach or coach students to become competitive in tournaments. He then replied that several of my students have discussed that it would be motivating if I returned to competition. I was taken by surprise. At first, you don't know if you should be insulted by such a remark, especially coming from a beginner. How dare he think I should return back to competition after a successful career participating in nationally recognized venues? After I calmed down, I realized he was absolutely correct in being the teacher/mentor for the students. If I wasn't fully invested in the activity and setting new goals, why would they be sold on my instructional methods? I came out of retirement a month later and continued to compete along with my students at nationally ranked tournaments for several more years.

Bill Tom was a 1956 Olympian and still continued to set goals up until his passing at age 89. He won countless titles in senior sporting events nationally and internationally. Dr. Wayne Westcott holds two Lifetime Achievement Awards and continues to provide valuable research that changes the way our field provides ongoing education in strength training. Mentors are people who continue to set goals even after many accomplishments and accolades. This is an important characteristic of mentoring. To this day, I have my kinesiology students write a one-month goal and a one-year goal during the first day of a class. One of my former students emailed me several years back, saying he thought my index cards of filling out goals was "cheesy" when introduced on a first day of class. He wanted to let me know that it now provides a valuable tool for his high school students and thanked me for introducing him to this concept. It also becomes a form of accountability. The rule behind proper goal setting is that they should be measureable and obtainable. This way, it's just barely beyond your reach and moderate effort should allow you to accomplish these goals. A good mentor demonstrates this concept constantly and makes it look easy to the novice mentee. Master Kan, a fictional mentor character from the 1970s TV series *Kung Fu* stated to the young Grasshopper (student), "Quickly as you can, snatch the pebble from my hand and when you can, it will be time for you to leave." The young student makes several attempts to grab the pebble from Master Kan's hand and fails miserably. It takes young Grasshopper several years to work at snatching the pebble from Master Kan's hand and eventually succeeds. Every one of us is the "grasshopper" attempting to accomplish a major goal in order to "leave." After you leave, it will be time for you to set your next major goal toward achieving success in this field.

Values Opinions of Others

We have talked about the concept of having respect, being connected in the field, setting goals within the field, etc. Where is it stated that a person who is an expert, well known the field, and well accomplished should have the time or tolerance to hear back from others who might have a difference of opinions or another conservable viewpoint? Believe it or not, I have witnessed great mentors who seek out the advice of others as well as absorb the brunt of criticism, even though it might not be merited. It demonstrates humility and grace and even the great ones don't always exhibit this virtue. I learned a valuable lesson a few years ago when I went to see Dr. Wayne Westcott speak at a regional conference. I was excited to travel a few hours up the highway to visit and hear Dr. Westcott speak about some recent studies he had completed with senior strength training concepts. During his second podium presentation, another professor from a local university delivered a harsh comment regarding a term that was used during his presentation. I was hoping Wayne would shrug this off and ignore the slight inconvenience this caused. However, to my surprise Wayne thanked the professor for his viewpoint and promised that he would make a correction to his presentation as soon as he returned back from his trip. I was taken aback by this gesture. Here was an expert who has been honored numerous times by major organizations for his academic accomplishments and the author of 24 books. Why would he even want to bow down to someone who didn't even match up to his accolades? Then, it dawned on me after my initial shock wore off. This is the exact reason why Wayne Westcott was a mentor and why I sensed he was revered by this industry and by his critics. This is why I knew I had more work to perform in my areas of weakness. Accepting the opinions of others is not an easy task to complete. It takes fortitude and tolerance to endure those remarks that aren't the most pleasant at times. It was a valuable lesson I learned that day about myself and why it is important to accept criticism, regardless if they are respectful or meaningful as long as you use this to motivate yourself to become better in your field. Dr. Westcott was the class act that day and showed why he is recognized more for his selflessness than accomplishments.

Considered as a Motivator

A motivator is someone who can pose a form of influence upon a person or people in order to promote positive change within the discipline. So, what motivates you to do things you like to do? What motivates you to complete tasks that you really don't care for? Can this be a person and if so, could this person be your mentor? When I think about my own career, there have been times where the push to complete or to compete was intrinsic. I told myself stories or bits and pieces of thoughts to push myself to do something such as completing a research manuscript or data collection process. However, I also looked at the people who have personally mentored me and they also have mentored others like me in this field to perform at a level that was unimaginable. Motivation doesn't have to be done with words. A certain expression, a gift of gab, or other physical tools have worked on other people to be productive in the field. Another past memory that continues to motivate me was when I was invited to help Dr. Westcott present a seminar to personal trainers on the East Coast. The organization leader went to Wayne and inquired how much less they should pay me per diem since I was at a rank of an Assistant Professor and did not have the same accomplishments as Dr. Westcott did. Without any thought, Wayne said, "You will pay him the same rate as me since he knows more than I do." My jaw practically hit the floor as did the organization leader. I gave my best presentation that day, knowing I had someone who fully believed in my skills and knowledge. I have never forgotten that day and it continues to motivate me in the future to make a difference in the field of kinesiology.

Peer Mentors

What are peer mentors and how does one become selected as a peer mentor? Being among your classmates or fellow students, there are a few who tend to step up to the plate more so than others. The leadership characteristic is sought out with kinesiology faculty or staff members who are more than willing to get assistance with creating future leaders. We don't always have to place a sign on someone's shirt, advertising that you are a peer mentor. There will be times when certain programs initiate this leadership opportunity, especially within a student club or organization. I was preselected as a peer mentor when I was a junior in college. My academic advisor sent a formal letter stating I have been recognized as a student leader and asked if I would participate in becoming a "peer mentor" for the incoming freshmen? I did volunteer but I was confused since I was never told what my responsibilities were. If new kinesiology students were having a tough time transitioning to college life, I would be a potential contact person for them but I was never called or asked to perform any duties. The concept seemed logical to have a peer mentoring program but there was no structure to the idea. So, what is the major responsibility of peer mentors? Knowing what I have experienced and knowing what I now know, the answer is…there is none. Peer mentoring should be exhibited by example and not by having a title or being told that you are now a "peer mentor." No one needs to advertise this concept by having a name tag or being placed in a directory, saying you are a peer mentor for underclassmen. This is not very effective, in my opinion. When I was a freshman in college, I befriended a kinesiology classmate named Billy Nava who was a junior at the time. The college campus was 1,438 acres and offered a tram service to pick up students and provide a ride to the next set of buildings. One day, Billy and I needed to go to the Admissions Building to drop off an add slip. I saw the tram approaching and told Billy to hop on. Billy replied, "Go ahead and take the tram. I am a kinesiology major so I will walk and meet you there." As I rode the tram by myself, I thought long and hard about what he said. After that day, I never took the tram again. Billy was never called on to be a student mentor for the kinesiology department but I was "peer mentored" by Billy and have never forgotten the important lesson he taught me that day. You do not have to possess a title or be officially appointed to be a mentor to another classmate. All you have to do is lead by example and the rest is formality. Act the professional you want to be and others will follow your lead. This is the true calling of a peer mentor.

Sage Mentors

Bibliotheque Nationale, Paris, FranceArchives Charmet/Bridgeman Images

What advantages do senior faculty members have or the experienced members of the squad compared to the younger crowd? This chapter has discussed plenty of characteristics that most sage types should possess. Must they always have long, flowing gray hair down to the shoulders or beards that seem to point toward their chest? None of my mentors have fit this description so sage mentors do not have to have a certain physical look or elderly trait. What they must possess is not just experience and wisdom, but successful experience and applicable wisdom to provide you with insight that will help your career travels be less worrisome. Sage mentors are plentiful in our field of specialties in kinesiology; however, they don't advertise themselves. By starting early and using the information provided in these first two chapters, you gain the advantage of finding a proper mentor who will connect with your needs and style. Do you want someone who is considered a sage mentor bombarding you with emails, texts, phone calls and micromanaging your life if this is not your comfort level or style? Do you want a sage mentor to be distant, withdrawn, not returning your emails, phone calls, etc. when you really need guidance or advice? There is this fine line and it takes time to connect with certain individuals who you have this informal or formal arrangement on what is comfortable to each other's personality. During the start of my higher education teaching career, I was assigned "sage mentors" at every institution where I taught. These sages would never meet with me and neither person would have discussions of what my needs were and what our mutual expectations should be.

It was basically a formality to say every new junior faculty member had a "sage mentor" as was earlier discussed in peer mentoring. Here was this process that was in place to provide a valuable service but there were no organized steps to gauge its effectiveness. So, here are some basic steps to set this "sage mentorship" in place that should prove effective toward proper mentoring:

1. Once you have qualified a person to be your "sage mentor," find a time to seek permission from this person to see if he or she is available and open toward mentoring you.
2. Meet to draw out plans on how to comfortably connect (once a month, emails, phone calls, etc.).
3. Ask about past mentees and issues that were not successful and how to avoid conflicts between the mentee and sage mentor.
4. Set up parameters on the expectations of both parties from each other. If goals are not being met or personality conflicts start to arise, an exit agreement must be in place that either party can execute at any time.
5. Regardless of the outcomes of the mentoring process, both parties should agree to stay on good terms with each other, avoiding the inability to stay professional in the future.

Remember, your first selection might not always be the best selection. I have had past issues with a few "sage mentors" during my career and I wish I had proper advice on how to gauge the process of not just the selection process but the accountability of both parties. The great sages I have had undoubtedly make up for the past mentors who weren't able to develop a plan that would promote my success in this field. Take your time with this and proceed cautiously. Selecting the right advisors will prevent you from hitting potholes during your career travels in kinesiology. Best wishes toward obtaining minimal roadblocks as you discover your path for career success.

Pictured: My former undergraduate advisor and sage mentor, Dr. Lynne Emery

CHAPTER 3
Setting Proper Goals and Time Management Skills

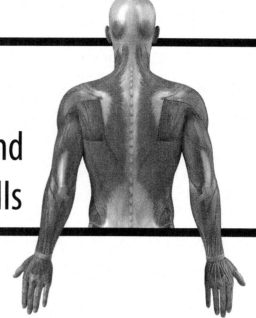

How many books have been printed or seminars given over the past 50 years on how to succeed by setting goals and obtaining the rewards, thus reaping the benefits of proper time management? After so many years and attempts, we still have people struggling with being successful in their career, not fully understanding why others will pass them up and leave them in the dust. One of the main reasons why certain people will further their career faster than other candidates is based on their vision. The vision is not just having a dream of being successful in the field of kinesiology; it is the ability to wear blinders like some race horses during the Kentucky Derby, but in a virtual sense. We all start off with the thought of pursuing a certain career path but along the way, potential roadblocks or potholes derail the path to accomplishing your eventual goals. I have unfortunately seen this with my fellow classmates, colleagues, and students. It's like that old cliché that we can lead a horse to water but you cannot make it drink. So, what are some tips that have worked for successful people as well as for me? This chapter will focus on some areas that can work for you, if you will take the time to drink the water, once you get to the watering hole.

How Does One Start Goal Setting in This Field?

Setting proper goals is considered an art form. Not everyone fully understands the ramifications of performing this. In past courses I have taught, I usually start with the introduction of general goal setting, using the concept of short-term and long-term goals. They don't have to be associated with kinesiology or career goals. It is just putting the wheels in motion to begin the process. The best way to teach goal setting is selecting something that needs to be completed or finished within a month. It is best to write this down somewhere where you can see this on a daily basis. The bathroom mirror, the front of a refrigerator, on a folder, daily planner, or your phone works well as a constant reminder to get something done. Once you have completed this task within 30 days, it is important to start the wheels in motion by setting up another goal immediately. By the end of the 30-day period, I usually introduce the next step, called the Career Success Pyramid (Figure 3.1).

Figure 3.1: Career Success Pyramid

This pyramid structure provides a proper guide as long as each goal is related to the past one, starting with the top 20-year goal. For example, let's start with the top lifetime goal. As an entry college student, you want to be the owner of a physical therapy practice as your top career goal. In order to be in this position, you must forecast that, at the 10-year mark, you are a practicing licensed physical therapist, working on professional business networking and researching the capital needed, in order to be able to own and run your business within 10 years. In order to be in this position at the 5-year mark, you must be enrolled in an accredited physical therapy program and maintaining good grades and asking the faculty about the pros and cons of owning your own physical therapy business vs. working for someone else. In order to be in this position within 1 year, you should be meeting with a good academic advisor to arrange your prerequisites, maintaining good grades with your undergraduate studies while staying focused on getting accepted into an accredited physical therapy school. This diagram becomes a mapping of your kinesiology career. A laboratory version can be found at the end of this chapter to get you started toward setting proper goals and getting a step closer toward your career success.

Time Management Skills

Why do certain people wait until the last minute to complete an assignment, or worst-case scenario, do not complete tasks that were promised to you or others? Would you agree that this particular characteristic would not be an admirable trait of a current or future student as well as a potential professional? It is important to promote a behavior that will be desirable and valuable to future employers. Setting this example in the classroom allows the professor to determine the type of person you want to present. It is also important to consistently promote this outside the classroom, even though you may not think it would be recognized or appreciated. Keeping a clean and organized desk does not equate to proper time management skills. I have met plenty of professionals who have a very organized office but there was no correlation with their ability to get things done within a certain timeline. It's based on attitude, not just an appearance of looking organized. Your attitude of getting things done within certain time constraints is based on your past success, motivation, and having cues available to reinforce this behavior. Rewarding yourself after each successful completion of a task is very important to serve as a positive reminder of continuing with this behavior. Let's start with how one can develop an attitude of success.

Intrinsic vs. Extrinsic Stimuli

Intrinsic motivation is developed by your own desires or pleasures. It can be a feeling you have developed that can lead to a form of happiness or self-satisfaction. There are many people who are self-driven to complete certain tasks based on these inner feelings. A sense of accomplishment or the feeling that you did the right thing are good examples of what motivates people to complete tasks. What allows college students to thirst for more knowledge? It could be the satisfaction of learning valuable information that led to an epiphany or "ah ha" moment. This moment should be seized and taken advantage of through intrinsic stimuli. The more these feelings are taken advantage of, the greater your ability to replicate this more easily in the future. A taste of this can motivate one to further this behavior of getting tasks done compared to those who cannot become motivated. I have colleagues or close friends who have asked how I am able to push myself to become an "over-achiever." I really do not consider myself an "over-achiever." When I have to come up with an explanation of why I am able to complete goals in a timely manner, I believe it is due to a habit of taking advantage of intrinsic cues. I firmly believe that everyone on this planet has the same and equal opportunity as anyone else, regardless of socio-economic levels or family upbringing. There are poor under-achievers and rich under-achievers in our society. Just because someone is raised in a disadvantaged neighborhood does not equate to failure. I have had plenty of inner-city students who have told me of their rough upbringing. When I asked why they chose to go to college and stick with an academic program vs. dropping out, their replies were very similar. They know part of the recipe for success is to leave the ghetto through educational means. Intrinsic motivation is a strong denominator to deflate peer and societal pressure allowing you to succeed or fail like many in similar situations choose to do. We will discuss sport psychology or wellness coaching as a kinesiology profession in later chapters. Intrinsic motivation is an interesting concept that is studied in depth since this concept is such a strong tool to use with clients. Finding ways to utilize this inner drive can be so powerful in helping you toward pursuing your goals and eventually accomplishing your career dreams.

Extrinsic motivation is found through outside sources compared to intrinsic methods. Beyond the intrinsic gains of gratitude or the thrill and enjoyment of performing are the external tangible effects such as winning an award or form of honor. A gold medal or earning a title of being the "Most Outstanding" Award winner are examples of being motivated by extrinsic means. Notice how different these things are compared to intrinsic means. However, both are able to get you to the next level, if used wisely.

So, intrinsic vs. extrinsic motivational techniques, which one is better for you? Past research studies performed by licensed psychologists have noticed that excessive use of extrinsic motivators could possibly reduce the internal motivators over a period of time, especially when the intrinsic motivators were allowing you to complete these tasks. For example, if you are rewarding yourself with a small gift for completing homework assignments compared to completing the assignments based on the enjoyment of the course, you could lose interest in performing the assignments after a period of time due to this conflict of feelings. This could result in poor performance since you no longer are doing a great job, based on enjoying the course though you are still rewarding yourself with a gift. On the flip side, extrinsic motivators could work in the opposite way by stimulating a person to perform something that was of no interest to you originally, but you completed the assignment on time since the reward was beneficial to the person. This could eventually take away the natural enjoyment of performing a task. It is highly recommended that external motivators be used conservatively compared to intrinsic ones. Once you have learned a new skill or have developed an appreciation for performing the task through external means, a person could develop an intrinsic connection to continue to pursue the activity if you can find personal enjoyment as your motivator.

Rewards Concept

Rewards can be very useful toward helping you reach your goals if used correctly. These external stimulators or physical attractors can help jump-start a new behavior or activity. A reward is a tangible product that acts as a reinforcement tool to start and/or continue toward completing a goal. Such tangible goods could be money, or a physical item that represents a successful completion, called a trophy. Trophies are often confused with plastic or metal figurines or statues we have often seen for athletic competitions. However, since our goal setting issues aren't always physically based toward athletic competitions, a trophy could even be a picture or drawing that represents an accomplishment. I have several framed pictures I place around my desk of my former students. A few years back, a reporter from the local newspaper wanted to visit and interview me for a feature story in the Lifestyles section. He was questioning me on my interests in the field of kinesiology and what got me there as a profession. He inquired about my athletic background and wanted to know the types of trophies or medals I have won from past tournaments or contests. Without pausing, I pointed to three small but professionally framed pictures of student group shots. I said, "These pictures are my trophies from my past accomplishments." He gave me a puzzled look and did not understand what that meant. I knew this could be a learning moment for a newspaper reporter so I let him know that I feel great satisfaction when I have students who I have invested time, energy, and patience towards having them become productive leaders in the field of kinesiology. He finally started to understand what these pictures represented. Instead of relying on a plaque that states some form of accomplishment within your career, the ability to create future leaders of tomorrow was just as good, or even better than having a large plastic cup sitting on my desk, collecting dust over time. He smiled when I said my former students are not collecting dust right now.

On the flip side, when rewards are used as motivational tools, it can backfire in regards to learning about what a trophy truly represents. I will share another story on how trophies can be misread or abused. At a recent national contest, one of my students made the evening finals and was competing for the all-around champion title. He ended up losing a very close and controversial bout to a person who he has defeated several times in past contests. His anger was focused on the second-place trophy, a much shorter piece of metal he was awarded during the ceremonies as well as the controversial judging. He also was upset since he wasn't given a point at the last second of the match and felt he deserved the six-foot first-place trophy. I carefully took him aside and asked if he gave his best performance tonight. He couldn't respond to my question so I said, "If you really feel you deserved to have the six-foot trophy, let's get in the car and go to the trophy store. I will buy you a six-foot trophy and you can display it at your house for others to ogle at. Will you really feel proud of displaying this trophy based on your performance tonight?" Finally, he understood about why I don't place a lot of value on physical rewards unless you truly earned it. Some of my old trophies sit in a box, collecting dust because I did just enough to win but I knew I didn't earn the reward. Rewards are only meaningful if you gave your full effort and your hard work resulted in a physical reminder. After a while, simple physical reminders such as a picture or a quoted phrase can stimulate intrinsic motivators without relying on tangible goods such as trophies or cash prizes to help complete a goal. The eventual goal is to achieve self-satisfaction, a feeling of worthiness based on a sense of accomplishment. This is a truly powerful product that can only be produced by your true efforts and not purchased at a drugstore or through a mail order. Winning a million-dollar prize based on an accomplishment might make you feel great but only for a short period of time. Having the feelings of earning this intrinsic "feel-good" is more valuable than your million dollars because the feeling you experience will last longer than the physical prize you have received.

Review and/or Reflections

Earlier in this chapter, it was discussed that there should be a period where reviewing of your progress takes place. This is important to make sure adequate progress is being made toward fulfilling your goal, both the short- and long-term ones. I can compare this to a commercial gym membership. As a new member, if you are fortunate enough to have a workout plan created to fit your goals, many members are not able to get another review to see how they are progressing. Goals need to be reassessed every 30 to 45 days to keep your motivation strong and clear. If you are not making progress within 30 days, there is still time to make adjustments to your behavior and use some tools mentioned in this chapter to keep you focused on the eventual prize. Review and reflection should still take place even if you meet your goals because you could identify issues that could be improved as your progress continues toward the next goal. For example, let's say your 30-day goal was to lose a half inch off your thighs so the program consisted of a four-day-per-week exercise program that included a lot of running. Eventually by sticking to this workout routine, you met your 30-day goal but it caused your Achilles tendon to flare up and brought pain and discomfort along the way. By reflecting on the type of path taken to achieve this goal, the idea of cross-training on alternative days using non-impact exercises could have gotten you to your goal but without the issue of creating the injury. Also, reflecting on if you are going towards the wrong direction could be identified sooner if you are charting your progress. Let's say your long-term goal was to gain acceptance into a law school within the next five years in order to become a licensed attorney. Through reflections of where you started with your goals and the progress you have made, you recognized that becoming a lawyer and working your way up the ladder was not as exciting as you thought earlier. Reassessing allows you to revise your career goals, re-establish your pyramid timelines, and direct your energies toward a career that you now can recognize as being your passion to pursue. The thought of going after your dream style fantasies of selecting a career from out of the blue could be made into major motion picture over several decades. Yes, dropping what you are currently doing and pursuing your new dream is truly a fantasy and but not very realistic. Do not be the waiter at the seafood restaurant in Maui who left on vacation from Pittsburgh, Pennsylvania, and decided not to return to the old job, based on the short-term excitement of living in Hawaii. I have seen and heard lots of examples of these knee-jerk career changes without thoughtful planning, leading to a successful outcome. Be the one who does the homework and follows the proper roadmap to success. Use the lab associated with this chapter to help guide you to achieving your overall success, especially in this career field. If your goal is to operate and own a successful surf shop in Maui, allow your adrenaline to become those intrinsic motivators for proper planning through short-

and long term goal setting. The first one on the beach doesn't necessarily win the race, but it's the one who can stay on the beach the longest and prosper from performing the homework. Proper reflections are necessary toward obtaining what others have only dreamt about but failed miserably due to ignoring these important tools.

Road Blocks and Potholes

As you travel down the road of life, you may see a sign ahead that says "roadblock." We have all seen these types of signs on the highway or country road but when it happens as you pursue your career, what should you do? First of all, you must determine if this barrier is truly external or internal. You will meet successful people on a regular basis and every one of them has experienced these challenges along the way toward achieving success. The secret is not how to avoid road blocks but how to navigate around them. What are you going to do when a financial issue or a poor grade will prevent you from moving forward? During my early college days, I had a string of road blocks fall right in front of me and who was there to give me advice? It was the same guy who wouldn't ride the tram with me and who taught me a valuable lesson about role modeling; but this time, when I vented to Billy Nava about the inability to pay for my required textbooks and get the classes I needed, his reply was, "If there's a will, there's a way." I probably gave him an unflattering look when he said this to me because it wasn't the advice I was seeking nor was it going to quickly fix my problems. When I asked how that statement was going to help me, he repeated with the same exact phrase. Of course, I wasn't in the mood to argue but reflecting back on what he said, he was again correct with his synopsis of my road block. So, what can you do to minimize road blocks or constant potholes that will always appear out of nowhere to deter your accomplishments of achieving your goals? Here are my answers, based on my experiences.

1. Reduce Negativity

How you manage stress, which increases during the initial stages of hitting a road block, is important. It's not uncommon to experience feelings of negativity, especially self-doubt, anger, and depression. Once these thoughts come out and visit you regularly, focus on the last event when you overcame such feelings. Remind yourself of how you went through similar feelings and how easy it was to take the path of misery vs. picking yourself up and dusting the negative thoughts from your system. Mantras work if you allow them to work for you. Hence, the Billy Nava method of repeating "If there's a will, there's a way" does work if you are willing to believe in this as well as pursue proactive methods to bypass road blocks. Reminding yourself of the road block is very ineffective toward removing these barriers. Strategize different paths to pursue that are positive in nature and keep using a mantra of working through the issue. Eventually, the barrier is either removed or bypassed without any additional damage toward completing your goal.

2. Eliminate Procrastination

There are times when the road blocks are self-imposed based on the inability to meet timelines, or completing a goal within your stated timelines. The stress of being constantly late, completing the assignment partially, or the inability to perform a quality performance comes from the attempt of trying to be perfect or the fear of becoming successful. Yes, it sounds strange but many times these are causes for not adhering to the standards you have set for yourself or what society had placed upon others to be successful in a career or in life. Make attempts to reduce procrastination by admitting to yourself and others that you aren't perfect. This announcement takes the burden off your shoulders and reduces the amount of stress. The feelings of nervousness and anxiety really won't go away until you minimize this negative habit. As an undergraduate student in kinesiology, only commit to projects or courses you are able to handle. Only you know yourself better than others. Having a computerized calendar or daily planner does not solve this issue unless you use it consistently. Your to-do list should be eliminated on a regular basis without this ability to add on to the existing list until tasks have been completed. As you are completing your daily tasks, the concept of procrastination becomes part of your past and no longer a part of your future.

3. Seek Support from Family and Friends

Do you have a network of people who you can vent your frustrations to? Are they supportive toward your career goals? If so, road blocks aren't eliminated by having friends or family who support you. They provide the ability to refocus on your barrier and to serve as a reminder of how important it is to continue through the struggle. Be cautious of those so-called friends or support networks who state they have your back but make attempts to sabotage your success based on their own failures. Beware of people who have hit their own road block and have not been able to bypass their issues so they would rather place their energies to road block others. These are the people to avoid until they are able to motivate themselves. Here is where a good mentor or sage mentor fits when you hit road blocks. They tend to provide the best advice and answers to your frustrating questions based on their past experiences. Seek these people out.

I've traveled down several career paths that have been blocked for certain reasons. The easiest solution is to pull over and wait until someone or something opens the blocked road or turn your car around and drive back to where you originally started. Detours can be effective only and if you slightly deviate your path away from a road block and can still make progress toward your goal. A good example of this concept is based on my own undergraduate experiences. After hitting several road blocks, ranging from being homesick as a freshman to having financial issues later as a junior, my friends and family kept reminding me of my goal to complete my studies. I remember my final road block toward completing my undergraduate degree in kinesiology and health promotion at Cal Poly Pomona. I was several hundred dollars short from paying my tuition fee to complete my last quarter. I received my mailed reminder to meet with my faculty academic advisor, Dr. Lynne Emery. As she verbally celebrated my last quarter to fulfill my degree, I sadly told her I would be taking the next quarter off due to financial issues. She replied that one of the classes I needed for graduation was only being offered once a year and to miss this class would result in pushing my graduation to the following year. I let her know I was prepared to deal with this road block and would not give up on finishing my studies, even if this meant I would wait another year for that last class. Without hesitating, she reached towards her purse and pulled out her checkbook and starting writing the amount I needed to pay for my classes. As I protested over and over again, she said she was not going to allow me to sit out another year and that she knew I would eventually pay her back. As I left her office that day, it finally hit me about how fortunate I was to have this type of academic advisor while other classmates had advisors who would only spend a few minutes going over their next classes and send them out the door. It took me six months but I worked an extra job during the summer after graduation to have enough money to repay this wonderful lady for her generous act. Once in a while, you will find someone or something that breaks down road blocks as long as you were willing to stay positive about the event.

4. Proactively Look to Improve Your Vision

Lack of preparation can lead to additional road blocks in one's pursuit toward a successful career. Besides the academic preparation, it is also the professional networking. There are no free rides or handouts in our profession. You must be sound with your foundations, especially knowledge based and experience savvy. Internships that provide a form of recognition that differentiates yourself from other candidates or volunteerism that could possibly pay off towards making you a better candidate reduce career road blocks. Obtaining a career in the kinesiology field requires more than a piece of paper showing a four-year degree. The stakes are higher and all kinesiology programs are different from each other. By understanding these variables, you are able to make better sense of what is needed to prepare for the competition when you complete your degree against other students from other institutions. This is a very competitive field and rightfully, it should be. Preparation at an earlier stage proves that you can avoid not all but some road blocks that will appear in the distant future.

5. Modify Your Program to Deflect Conflicts

Another suggestion to avoid the pitfalls of certain potholes and road blocks is to review your progress annually. In my experience as a former kinesiology student and current professor in this field, I have seen numerous kinesiology students change their specialty yearly. This is really a common phenomenon and not surprising since I can remember that I did the same thing also. I started out wanting to be an athletic trainer and ended up specializing in corporate fitness by the time my undergraduate studies were completed. I had lots of help along the way, from my upper classmates to my academic advisor who would point out potential road blocks if I pursued a certain program as a kinesiology career. It is helpful to have a draft of your academic program posted and reviewed on a regular basis. Once you do decide to change direction towards another major or specialty, you are able to best make the decision how to navigate and still continue to make progress. Your academic advisor would be your first visit after confirming your change of directions. Parents and friends sometimes can supply incorrect information about kinesiology careers. It's best to bring these concerns to your academic advisor since inaccurate information will create a road block.

6. Maintain an Active Lifestyle

Taking time to take care of your physical needs is not a cure to roadblocks but it doesn't hurt. In fact, it can achieve several functions. First, you demonstrate your goal of maintaining a level of fitness by not neglecting this component. Second, proper exercise is a stress reducer and can help to temporarily relieve some of the "fight or flight" activators which accompany the stress response. Thirdly, the results of promoting this can clear some of the mental cobwebs and allow you to make a reasonable judgment vs. an irrational emotional one that could come back to haunt you later. I wish exercise was the "cure all" to all road blocks and stress responses, but it's not. It provides a temporary fix and allows a period of calm to set in and allow you a period of relief before the external stimuli come back to remind you again on why you are going through a road block. Then, the stress response resumes again. A combination of using biofeedback as well as physical exercise seems to work as a complimentary stress reducer than just physical exercise. Yoga or martial arts that incorporate breathing exercises, visual cueing, and reframing activities work very well and incorporate the physical routine at the same time. Determining what fits your personality as well as convenience will determine which path is best for you to use this as a road block demoter.

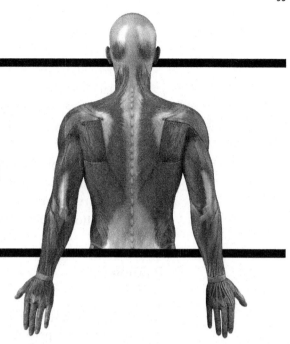

CHAPTER 4
Beginning Your Path in Kinesiology

So far, we have discussed how common it could be changing your mind a few times, deciding what specialty is right for you in this field of kinesiology. Besides that, I have also confused you toward thinking about who would be a good mentor as well as the pressure of being a peer mentor at the same time. Another factor toward reaching for success is forcing you to select career goals by starting at the top of the pyramid and working your way down in order to figure out what steps are needed and the time elements that must be associated with your success. Of course, to make this work, you must develop proper time management skills and prepare to navigate from potholes or have a plan of attack when road blocks are being faced during your journey.

I know how one would feel if given all of this detail in a short period of time. It's best to start planning accordingly at this early stage and letting you know how this challenging journey can be so rewarding as long as you have a general overview of what it takes to be successful in this career field. Are you now ready to start the journey? Let's start by selecting a specialty in kinesiology and going from there. Once you have selected this, it's time to see what you can do to determine if it's the right fit for you.

Recognizing Job Characteristics

There are 10 variables that should be considered when deciding what type of career you would like to pursue in the field of kinesiology. After reviewing each of these variables, do you think the direction you are heading in will fit with what you eventually would like to become? Let's review each one more carefully before deciding.

1. Passion
2. Personality (group or individual settings) (slow or high paced)
3. Salary/money
4. Benefits/retirement package
5. Work environment hours
6. Job security
7. Upward mobility within the company
8. Location and availability
9. Industry growth and need
10. Education and/or certifications (CEUs)

Passion

Passion is the positive, exciting feeling you have when experiencing an opportunity that continues for a period of time. This feeling should transfer to the occupation you decide to partake in, especially if you intend to pursue this as a career goal. Most people would consider a career to last longer than 20 years since most retirement systems use this as a marker of longevity in many occupations. Passion about a certain career path can be based upon an experience you had previously or something that happens to bring a rush of adrenalin when thinking about the topic. I have heard several stories of former students who selected physical therapy as their career path based on a past accident or injury they suffered in high school. After going through sessions with a physical therapist, a connection develops between the patient and the occupation, especially after spending numerous hours of seeing a physical therapist in action. The concept of helping people becomes a strong influencer of developing a passion for this type of work. Notice how this connection took place through the interactions of patient to healthcare provider. Are there specific roles you see in kinesiology that would bring this excitement to your daily routines? This would be the start of exploring if you can transfer this energy to the job site.

Personality

Personality is the ability for a person to respond to his or her environment. It is forgotten that one's personality does play a role in being successful in certain kinesiology professions. For example, if you are an introvert, teaching group classes or attempting to motivate members to exercise in a corporate setting would be challenging. Introverts tend to do well in clinical settings or with one-to-one personal training scenarios. However, you cannot change one's personality but can modify behavior. If you truly want to pursue a certain career field that requires public speaking, changes in behavior can help overcome one's personality. It was very difficult for me personally to lead an exercise class. I remember several professors who were instrumental toward pushing me to leading warmups in group settings. Once I realized that no one was making fun of me or criticizing my methods, each additional day of leading the class became less stressful. I still consider myself an introvert but over the years, I have given hundreds of speeches without any hesitation. I have learned to wear special hats when I present to large groups or audiences. If you do have a quiet, soft-mannered personality, learning to change your behavior can result in successful public speaking and the successful pursuit of kinesiology careers that require this trade.

Salary/Money

If the question is, "Can I make a decent living from this type of career?" the answer should be a resounding "yes." It's just that depending upon the type of job and amount of experience you have, salaries are going to vary just like other academic fields. For the first career job offer, salary is an important factor. Can you maintain financial independence from others who you relied on to pay the bills, rent, car, etc.? Salaries will always be higher in the clinical fields than non-clinical, but the amount of education also dictates the salary scale. A kinesiology degree with the right specialization and added certifications and/or credentials opens up more doors that are willing to pay you for what you are worth. I ask my advisees on a regular basis, "What is going to make you more valuable than all the other candidates from neighboring colleges or universities who are claiming they are just as qualified as you"? The more skills you possess, the more money you will make. This needs to be embedded when you take your core classes in the field. For example, how many of you can organize and run a successful golf tournament or a 5K run? You wouldn't think this type of skill would help your annual salary but think about it. If you are able to bring in revenue or participants to your employer, don't you think this would justify your salary or the ability to increase your salary quickly? Your past experience and employment history will also dictate how much money you can request. Everything is negotiable, especially your annual salary. Don't rush to take the first offer when given the opportunity to be the selected candidate. Once a job is offered, you are now in the driver's seat with a starting salary and other benefits. However, do not be disrespectful about the hiring process. Do your homework and look at comparable salaries from similar employers and use this as well as your experience or skills to justify your counteroffer. Also, be prepared to know when to cut your losses. Suppose this is the only existing opening in the area you would like to reside in. Do not turn down this entry-level job that can help catapult you to the next level within a year or longer. In most situations, the person offering you an annual salary will be respectful about the process, too. Be polite and professional and you will obtain the salary you deserve.

Besides the starting salary, are you familiar with the COLA issue or merit pay? COLA, also known as cost of living allowance, allows employees to increase their annual salary based on predicted inflation costs. Some companies allow for COLA to increase salaries over the next several years to keep up with living cost increases or to maintain current industry standards within the profession. Merit or performance pay is base salary increases due to your ability to improve current standards, quotas, or due to exemplary accomplishments. Knowing these incentives, a lower base or starting salary can be temporary and acceptable to you if you are able to know future expectations.

Benefits/Retirement Package

The topic of retirement or medical benefits is usually not a top priority when introduced after considering a job or position within a company. When I got my first job offer at the First Interstate Bancorp to be an exercise specialist for their corporate fitness program, I was more enthralled with the annual salary. When the human resource representative gave me options for medical, dental, and retirement benefits, I declined or took the bare minimum, because I felt I wouldn't need medical or other benefits since I was pretty healthy and felt immortal. This was a major mistake and I am fortunate that I was able to recover from this errant judgment a year later. Sometimes health and retirement benefits can make up for a lower annual salary. If given an opportunity, study the benefit package of the company or employer who is hiring you. I was fortunate to realize how important these issues are, even though retirement seemed so far away. Invest in your future now and you will thank yourself for being proactive and visionary. This goes with medical and health benefits. Don't be that person who does not have adequate health insurance when it's needed. Be smart and realize that your climb up the corporate or success ladder will pay off toward making a comfortable living while you are protected in other areas.

Work Environment Hours

One cannot always expect to work 9 to 5, Monday through Friday. My first corporate fitness job required that I open up the facility at 5:30 a.m., but I was able to leave by 2:30 p.m. which allowed me to have additional opportunities such as graduate school at night. If you aren't a morning person, if you want this type of job, you will learn to be one. During my freshman year, I had problems waking up for a 7 a.m. weight training class. Why was this so? Well, when I looked back upon my behavior, the concept of lifting weights at 7 a.m. had no meaning to me personally. There was no identified goal set or an understanding of why I needed to wake up early to lift weights. It just fit my schedule at the time so I signed up for it with the best intentions but because this class wasn't strongly identified as something that was a necessity, I "blew it off" and ended up dropping the class four weeks later. Yes, sadly I wasn't the best role model for others to follow back then. So, what's the moral to this story? If you say you're not a "morning person," it doesn't matter as long as know that many kinesiology professions will have morning preferences. There aren't too many jobs in this field that I can cite that are considered afternoon starts through the evening hours unless these businesses or facilities run past 8 p.m. daily. Changing behavior regarding working hours can create the ability to secure a good job, especially if the position is a great fit and can lead to other opportunities. Forecast this issue and speak with your supervisor if hours could change in the future once you establish job seniority.

Job Security

What is job security? This is the ability to keep or maintain your position until you decide to take another position of your choice in the future. Does one usually think about this concept when you are hired? The answer is usually no, unless someone or some concept comes up. It's just assumed that you will have your job until you decide to leave for another one. That is not always the case. My first experience with this topic arose when I was working a part-time position as an exercise instructor for the Pritikin Longevity Center during my senior year in college. I really enjoyed this position since the hours worked around my class schedule, it was close to my apartment, paid well, and provided the ability to showcase my skills learned from my kinesiology classes. However, I never asked the right questions or voiced concerns about job security. Within four months, the staff was given layoff notices for our center without much previous warning. This was an eye-opening experience for me since I was never aware of such issues occurring at a job site. Six months later when I received a job offer to work full time at a bank, performing corporate fitness, it was a question I did express since financial institutions do get taken over by other competitors on a regular basis. My question was answered that there was always a possibility of a hostile takeover by another institution but that we would be given six months' notice before anything would affect our job status. I was able to finish my master's degree during that time and leave for higher education before this bank was bought out four years later. My ability to look at the conditions of job security and be able to wisely parlay this into another kinesiology field was definitely 20/20 hindsight. Take care of your future by knowing what your job security will be at the worksite.

Upward Mobility

Upward mobility within the job site is another important factor to consider when selecting a profession. When I took on my first real kinesiology position at the bank, I didn't understand the idea of "moving up" in the organization. Quickly, I found out that my ability to be promoted at this worksite would be very limiting since there were only four of us in the corporate fitness division for this financial institution. Understanding this limitation did not deter my ability to perform well. It allowed me to rethink my options towards the future and I returned to school to increase my ability to have upward mobility in a different direction within a few years. You need to look not only at the type of kinesiology profession but also at the worksite. Not all positions have limited growth within the industry. It's dependent upon the company or worksite. A classmate of mine also started in corporate fitness at a small company. Instead of going back to graduate school for an advanced degree, he was able to network with other companies at national conferences. Within several years, he was a vice president of a nationwide fitness manufacturer. Currently, he is a senior vice president of a health club chain that has over 175 franchises all across the country. Every job move he made was a vertical move and that would be something of great advice to promote. Gone are those days where your mother or father stayed at the same employer for over 30 years based on comfort and loyalty. The culture of employment has changed over the past 25 years. It reminds me of the concept of free agency in professional sports. When I was a teenager, I would become upset when I heard a certain professional athlete was leaving the team who drafted the player out of college. I felt that this was a selfish move and unwarranted since this person should stay loyal to the team who selected this player. However, it started making more sense to me when I hit my first "glass ceiling" at my first teaching job.

A "glass ceiling" is an obstacle to a clear path towards upward mobility at the jobsite. An appearance of the ability to move upward through written policy or verbal commitment exists but you are not allowed to move forward for several reasons. One of those reasons may be the inability for your supervisors or upper management to adhere to the written policies for promotion. Another reason may be financial issues within the company, not allowing you to be promoted since the company is not able to provide the compensation for your advancement. Also, it could be the inappropriate use of "hidden deals" or agenda made to suppress certain people from being promoted in favor of other selected employees. Politics are everywhere, even in professional sports. When I hit this glass ceiling for the first time, I finally realized the value of free agency in professional sports. If I was to be promoted and compensated for my merits, it would have to be with a different team, regardless of loyalty of the institution for hiring me over others. Stay professional and productive while you shop for other employers who are willing to hire you for your skills and merits. The grass can be greener on the other side of the fence.

Location and Availability

Wouldn't it be perfect if you could just pick your location where you wanted to work and life would be so simple? Unfortunately, that's not how it works. Your chances improve in larger population cities, where the demand for kinesiology-related jobs is high. However, in smaller towns or rural areas, the demand is limited or not there. Recently, I had a parent discussing kinesiology as a major and if her daughter will find a job in a town with a population of 500 people. I told her if this was the case where the plan was to return to a small-town environment, becoming a nurse or dental hygienist would bring higher success of being hired in this scenario. Even if fitness or sport-related businesses were found in small communities, it would be difficult to obtain an entry-level position since most of these jobs are not transitional. What this means is that these employees do not leave the area and end up staying at this site much longer than usual. So, what does this mean for finding a job in this field? It means the understanding of having to go elsewhere to get your experience and having the understanding that you can come back eventually, once you have more experience and skills to offer when the opening is available. I will share another story of a former student of mine asking me why I left my teaching position in San Diego, California, for Pittsburgh, Pennsylvania. His rationale was, "How could someone leave such a beautiful place like San Diego?" My reply was originally validating his response: "Yes," I said, "who would want to leave such a beautiful place?" Then I realized this student was a former football player and I decided to ask him about the concept of free agency. I said, "If the San Diego Chargers drafted you as a running back but never gave you enough carries per game, wouldn't this bother you after a while?" He nodded his head in approval stating that a professional football career is unpredictable and getting the ability to prove your worth was very important. That is when I told him to compare this to what I do. I wanted the ball more often and when this doesn't occur with a certain team, I ask for a trade or attempt to sign on to another team who will realize my worth and give me the ball more often. This was why I left sunny San Diego and went to a much colder climate. As I stated before, once you get your needed experience and accomplishments, you have a higher probability to select the location of your choice as long as they have opportunities available for your specialty. Happiness can be derived by more variables than just sunshine and the ocean breeze, but it's not a bad spot to end up at if this becomes your eventual landing spot.

Industry Growth and Need

How familiar are you with the industry needs for your current career interest? Are you familiar with the projected growth and availability for the increased workforce? When I started as a kinesiology and health promotion major, I had no clue about the industry needs. I just expected like most other students that once you finished all your coursework, you would start applying for jobs that were related to the major. Looking back, it wasn't the best approach to take but times were a bit different back then. The Internet was not available so it was very tough to perform research at the library or to rely on professors who always weren't connected to the present or future needs of the discipline. These days, students have greater access and visibility to what is trending or being forecasted towards finding a lucrative career. There are lots of reference materials that will allow you to know if there are plentiful jobs in your area. From yearly reports from national periodicals to certain industry sites available on the Web, it's important to note that dependent upon the source, it's best to see if the information is legitimate and from citable sources. One of the ways I was able to extract information back in my day was to inquire the graduating seniors who were applying for jobs in the industry. This was not only helpful, it allowed me to start making changes to the curriculum I was taking in order to secure a possible job when I graduated. However, just because national trends would state the need for underwater basket weavers who can hold their breaths for five minutes in the next several years, lacking the enjoyment, passion, and drive to perform this job for 20 plus years could be depressing. Yes, it's important to know in the beginning what your chances will be in securing a job in your specialty as you pursue your coursework. I know college friends who were art majors during my undergraduate studies and to this day are unable to secure a job in this profession even though they are very passionate about the field. It's something to keep in mind. On the flip side, I am also convinced if the passion and excitement is there for a certain profession, you will always find your niche as long as you are willing to travel where the job is available, regardless of current industry needs or trends.

Education and/or Certifications

It's obvious that an accredited college degree in kinesiology or something similar is necessary to be eligible for a relevant job in the field. It also must be assumed that the type of coursework taken and related certifications would be necessary to assist with this opportunity. Be warned that not all kinesiology degrees are created equal. From an outsider's perspective, you would assume so but this is not true for all institutions nationwide. Make sure your coursework is applicable towards what is needed for your career. If you are not sure about this, check job descriptions and responsibilities of potential advertisements in trade journals or on recognized organizational websites that offer job announcements. Having a kinesiology degree geared more toward a general recreational supervisory position would not be a good fit if you wanted to pursue personal training. As you progress towards graduation and decide what would be an ideal career, this would be the time to pursue a certification. A personal training license or certification would make up lost coursework you did not get while taking non-exercise-related classes. The reason for waiting near the end of your studies to pursue this is twofold: (1) The costs associated with most well-known certifications are not lenient for one's pocketbook. So, it's best to know which exam to take before committing the costs associated with having this added perk. Many of these certifications will run between $260 and $400. As we progress through the different specialties in kinesiology, the specific information on proper certifications will be covered in these upcoming chapters in the text. (2) During the junior to senior level of your studies, you have probably made some changes to your ideal career direction and have a better viewpoint of what is needed to secure a good entry-level job. I made several changes between my freshmen through senior year of my chosen specialty so this is another reason to wait a bit longer before committing to any extra coursework and/or certification process.

There will be professions besides a licensure or certification necessary to obtain legal employment. An advanced degree may be something you want to also start to think about, especially if you want to move up the career ladder a bit faster than others (i.e., MBA degree for the sport management specialty or to qualify for clinical professions such as DPT [Doctor of Physical Therapy] or MOT [Master of Occupational Therapy]). Once you finish your undergraduate degree, there isn't a rest break or pause for most students who decide to pursue this route. This would be another reason to keep up your overall grades. You never know if you will pursue graduate school and if so, most programs do require at least a 3.0 and qualifying graduate entrance exam scores (i.e., GRE, MAT, or GMAT). If you decide to pursue K-12 public school teaching, additional coursework will be needed, as well as a six-month to one-year residency program for student teaching at several sites. Passing state licensure examinations are necessary to earn your teaching certificate. However, every state will have different requirements and steps to perform. Private PK-12 institutions do not have to have these requirements for teachers or coaches but you would want to inquire since some would have this policy intact. Higher education will most likely require a graduate degree in the field of study. Most community colleges or junior colleges will require a master's degree in the discipline you intend to teach. Community college teaching credentials used to exist until the early 1990s in certain states. All of these credentials were eliminated at this level by the mid-1990s and the master's degree has replaced this. For four-year colleges or universities, a terminal degree will be required to work at this level even though a master's degree is considered for some institutions if research is not a requirement.

Student Clubs and Professional Memberships

Does belonging to and being a student member of a particular club or organization help toward getting a job? I believe it does have merit so I have included it and hope to justify its relationship with obtaining your first career job in the industry. If we talk about student clubs that are readily available to join, it's a sign of social progression among your fellow students. It demonstrates being involved even if it is a religious group or honor society. Now, in order to strengthen your ability to connect with certain employers or companies, joining a professional organization as a "student member" shows commitment to the field of study. It could be the sport management or exercise science club, but you also want to make sure the student club has a connection to the professional national or international organization via a charter or affiliation. If you aren't sure, ask your club president or faculty advisor for clarification. Also, most to all major national organizations allow individual students to join as "student members" for a nominal fee. This is a clear demonstration that you are connected to your field and committed to keeping up with the latest information or trends in the industry. Sometimes the cost of membership can be detrimental since most of us are poor college students. The amount for student membership is minimal at the local level. The professional memberships are a bit higher but still generally affordable ($40 to $60/year). I joined numerous clubs on campus as an undergraduate and graduate student. Not only did I find this helpful but quite eye-opening since I had no formal leadership background as a college student. Companies, organizations, and facilities don't always advertise this concept but everyone looks for leaders or potential leaders. So, besides joining and participating in the process of representing a student group, take on responsibilities that showcase your leadership skills.

As another important aspect of student club participation, I would also encourage the leadership role by running for an elected office or position. This could be within the student organization first. Branching out to being the voice of the students in a professional organization is a big deal. It is not easy to win these seats or positions and if you do, it is a great resume builder and can open more doors for you within that professional organization. Check the organization's webpage and profile to see how often they vote in student representatives and the qualifications towards winning this seat. Carpe diem......seize the moment!!

Internships or Cooperative Experiences/Volunteerism

This concept is so important that I really think without my co-op experiences, I would have selected the wrong specialty and profession. Co-ops and internships are related and can be quite different in their original interpretation. Co-ops are structured learning-based experiences based on curriculum being taught in specific classes. There is a theoretical concept behind cooperative experiences having a service learning integration concept at a jobsite. If you were able to take skills learned in the classroom and apply this to current problems at the worksite, this form of experiential learning forms the basis of cooperative education. In my case, I had the opportunity to perform three cooperative experiences during three different semesters while at Cal Poly University. I never formally participated in an internship during my undergraduate days.

These days, internships have replaced co-op experiences in the majority of kinesiology curriculum nationwide. Internships are considered on-the-job training at the physical location or facility. It sounds very similar to a co-op but there really isn't a formal service learning concept. It's basically a practice place to learn while you volunteer your time at the worksite. The majority of internships in kinesiology programs are unpaid compared to other majors. Why is this so? It is due to the inability of the majority of students to go into a worksite and develop a product or concept that will lead to the company making money in a short period of time. A good example was when I did my last co-op at General Dynamics in Pomona, California. General Dynamics was a defense contractor for the Navy and my job was to supervise and facilitate their 10,000 employees to use the fitness facilities before, during, or after scheduled work hours. I was not developing a new product or system for them. I was there to gain work experience and learn how their fitness center functions as a corporate fitness concept. On the flip side, my friend Ted performed an internship at the same place but as an electrical engineer intern. He was paid for his internship time since his role was to improve circuit board function and commands of the Titan 2 rockets that were attached to the U.S. Navy submarines. These were skills that Ted already possessed and it made sense why he was paid to produce a product. Regardless, the experience I received and the amount of time I put into this co-op did pay off. If I didn't have this experience, there was no way I would have qualified for the corporate fitness opening a few months later. The bank that hired me said that was a major factor on why I was selected over other candidates who performed a co-op or internship at a fitness facility but was not considered corporate in nature. The concept of corporate fitness will be covered later in the text vs. other programs that would be considered as a corporate fitness program, so don't panic if you aren't totally sure about this concept.

The hours of service differ per program. It's a commitment and shows full-time service when an internship will go over 400 hours during the semester. Think about the skills you could develop or learn if you find an internship that will allow you to work over 400 hours of detailed skill development vs. just 120 hours of shadowing or following people through their daily routines. Don't think that unpaid internships are unfair and not worthy. If you are able to learn valuable skills that you would not have received in the classroom, it is worth the effort and time. Once in a blue moon, there will be paid internships for kinesiology students but they are extremely rare and competitive. This would be another reason why students should get involved with student-run clubs within the major. These internship sites want the "best of the best." These best students have a high GPA, are involved with student clubs, probably have an elected position in a club or professional organization, and are connected with a professor who has strong ties to the industry. These go-getters are the ones who will be selected for the paid internships that are coveted by many students yearly. Are you able to portray a go-getter with your current background? As we have discussed, not all internships are created equal and considered convenient for your lifestyle. Many interns will travel across the country to have the opportunity to work with a well-known trainer or promoter while others will settle for finding something next door to them. I hope by reading into this important concept, you will realize besides the foundational skills you have learned in the classroom, the next biggest element will be the internship experience. Take this component extremely seriously when starting to plan your career.

Volunteering is more than being part of a student club or putting in extra time at a co-op or internship site. Volunteerism is a character issue that companies or programs look for without advertising or asking for this virtue. Graduate programs have been known to look for this characteristic without letting candidates know of the desire to recruit people that have this tendency of giving back to the community without the auspices of getting something in return. It doesn't have to be related to kinesiology at all. It's about the concept of "giving." Many research studies have confirmed that people who volunteer on a regular basis in their community are reliable, dependable, trustworthy, and have the ability to cope under stress compared to those who didn't perform this regularly. Performing this concept is not because you want to be a better employee or student; rather, volunteering comes from within and represents who you are. As I look back at several projects I volunteered in as an undergraduate, I merely did so in the beginning because of peer pressure. After a while, it became more than just a few friends saying it was the right thing to do. It became a mission because I learned to have ownership of the idea. Having a built-in mechanism that becomes an emotional knee jerk is passion. You want to volunteer because you have a cause to help a person, organization, etc. since there is a connection you have to this entity. It goes beyond resume building and fluffing your background in order to show more substance. What are some causes you are willing to burn the midnight oil to accomplish that you can organize a student or professional club to participate in? Are you able to generate interest from others because it is the right thing to do? Altruism, the ability to give back without asking for anything in return, is a strong dose of self-worth. Not only is this good for people's character building, it also improves the concept of being human. This also helps define who you are and what you represent. Wouldn't you want people to accept you for who you really are and what you proclaim you want to be? It certainly makes a better working environment if you can be yourself but you would want management to be accepting of you also.

Finding the right occupation and being the right fit isn't a mathematical formula or routine recipe. This chapter brought up many characteristics and important points to consider as you further your journey into selecting a career in kinesiology. The next several chapters will now delve into the specifics of these types of occupations and their own characteristics discussed by people who currently live through them today.

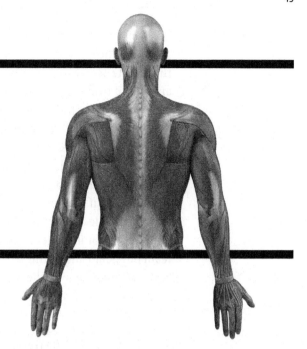

CHAPTER 5
Clinical Professions

These are medical or health professions that prepare individuals to practice as licensed professionals or assistants in the healthcare professions and related clinical sciences on patients or clients. In the field of kinesiology, this area has been very attractive to students seeking a role that deals directly in the medical field but allowing options of scope and the ability to enjoy choosing the desired workplace. In this chapter, we will not cover every single clinical profession that a kinesiology major could find a career with. This would not be practical, but we will focus on those professions that are common within the field of kinesiology today.

Athletic Training

The profession of athletic training has been formally around since the 1950s, even though there probably were similar functions for managers or even players back in the late 1800s when professional sports had its start in this country. The National Athletic Trainer's Association is the only organization for this profession and sets the standards and reinforces the scope of the athletic trainer since its inception in 1950. Since the beginning of the NATA, both the scope and practice of the athletic trainer have changed over the past several decades.

What Do Athletic Trainers Do?

A certified athletic trainer works in conjunction with many health and medical professionals. In the early days, the athletic trainer worked under the directions of the head coach or the coaching staff to assist with preparing the athlete for practice or game situations as well as to provide proper care to treat injuries and help rehabilitate the athlete to return to either the practice field or game situations in a reasonable amount of time, depending upon the injury or conditions of the environment. Nowadays, the athletic trainer works under the direction of a medical director or physician. According to the NATA website, the scope of practice among certified athletic trainers is to "provide preventative services, emergency care, clinical diagnosis, therapeutic intervention and rehabilitation of injuries and medical conditions." Many are also involved with strength and conditioning roles with athletes, depending where they are working and if they possess additional background or credentials to warrant such an additional role. Other roles of an athletic trainer include the educational component of advising not just clients, but patients, athletes, coaching staff, a medical team (e.g., team physician and administration). This position also includes certifying the support and staff members in the area of first aid, CPR, and the use of an AED (automatic electronic defibrillator).

Another important role is in the area of counseling or life coaching with patients or athletes. Many athletic trainers are the liaison between the coaching staff and the players. If any information is to be extracted regarding training or outside interferences, usually the athletic training staff can be privy to this important information. For example, eating disorders are unfortunately common in certain sports and athletic performance or injury recovery can be affected by such dangerous behaviors. The athletic trainer is usually a buffer between the athlete and the coaching staff and is able at times to intervene and counsel the participant to make certain behavioral changes that would not be adhered to if the coaching staff was delivering the message. A positive image and relationship plays an important role for athletic trainers besides just treating and evaluating sports injuries. The ability to be sought after for advice and motivation are within their scope of practice.

The remaining areas of responsibility are developing a good working relationship with your supervisor and team physician and providing accurate and concise reports. Developing a cohesive relationship with the team doctor and providing open communication are also crucial roles. Besides discussing the specific injuries and treatment options, the ability to share ideas or provide additional details about the patient on a regular basis is important to this position. Sometimes the involvement of working with patients or athletes becomes so time consuming and the administrative tasks of preparing and recording accurate and current information fall to the wayside. Even though these tasks are not very exciting, they are crucial toward providing record upkeep and demonstrating professionalism at all times. Think about it, would you want your paperwork to be shuffled around or unorganized at your physician's office? Of course not, so it's important to keep everything accurate and to demonstrate your ability to provide this data in an organized manner when called upon.

Examples of Athletic Training Positions of Employment

- Athletic Trainer, Healthcare Program
- Ambulatory Care Practitioner
- Clinical Athletic Trainer
- Clinical Manager - Satellite Clinics/ Athletic Health Care
- Club Sports Certified Athletic Trainer
- College Athletic Trainer
- College Assistant Athletic Trainer
- Combined Outreach Athletic Trainer
- Community Sports Team Clinical Athletic Trainer
- Director Occupational Health
- Director Rehab Therapy Services
- Exercise Specialty Clinical Athletic Trainer
- General Clinical Athletic Trainer
- Head Certified Athletic Trainer/ Clinic and Athletic Healthcare
- High School Athletic Trainer
- Hospital and Ambulatory Medical Center-based Certified Athletic Trainer
- Hospital-based Care Practitioner- Certified Athletic Trainer
- On-site Occupational Athletic Trainer
- Physician Extender - Clinical Athletic Trainer
- Program Director Role
- Secondary School Athletic Trainer

Source: (http://www.NATA.org)

Working Environments for Athletic Trainers

As you can see by observing the abovementioned types of athletic training positions, the working environment is diverse. Most likely, you will be in an area where the physical rehabilitation and evaluation will be on-site but for most entry-level positions, you will not stay situated on a regular 8 to 5 shift in one area. It will consist of indoor and outdoor environments with extremely non-stop business to waiting on the playing field until your services are needed. There will be a physical cost to your assignment as an athletic trainer since you could be standing for long periods of time, kneeling, squatting, sitting, etc. Most likely, there will be a travel component for most athletic trainers who are employed by sport teams, whether it be high school, college, or professional sports. Your days could run past 12 to 14 hours at times, especially when there is a scheduled competition that could last into the late evening hours. Usually, a set hourly schedule is given to those who are able to secure a clinic or outpatient setting at a hospital, usually given to those with seniority or more administrative credentials. Weekdays, weekends, early morning treatments, and late night games or contests are part of the world of the athletic trainer. If you really enjoy the responsibilities and the environment, the amount of hours needed really wouldn't make a difference since it's part of the life of being an athletic trainer.

Being able to handle all the physical and administrative tasks can take a toll over time. Stress-related issues are considered common especially in the healthcare field, when there are many sides to please—from the athletes or participants to your medical director, the head coach or coaching staff, the administration side or management team, to other athletic trainers, and the support staffers who you will work with directly or indirectly. Your ability to handle these relationship stressors as well as your performance issues can take a toll over a period of time if you are not prepared to handle the workload. Understanding your role and taking responsibilities for management of your stressors will ultimately decide if this job is for you. The goal is to have healthy clients and to maintain this status until you are told otherwise by your medical director. Competitive sports will always find a way to place more emphasis on winning than on maintaining someone's overall wellness. Are you able and ready to handle this? If so, this could be your career path.

Employment Outlook for Athletic Trainers

If you observe the United States Bureau of Labor Statistics (BLS), employment is steady among this career during the past several years. As of May 2013, there were 22,300 athletic trainers employed in the United States. The majority of athletic training employers were colleges, universities, or professional schools (n = 4,710). The next largest employers are hospital-based centers or outpatient clinics (n = 3,660). The lower 10% annual salary for a board-certified athletic trainer starts around $26,000 and caps around $66,000 annually at the 90% tier level. The average starting salary of any certified athletic trainer will always rely on experience, advanced degree completion, and other additional certifications that will be explained later in this chapter. The ability to seek out available jobs nationwide is dependent upon the need and availability. The majority of athletic training jobs are offered on the East Coast compared to the rest of the country. The lowest need is in the upper Midwest region of the country (Figures 5.1 and 5.2).

According to several unnamed sources of athletic training professors nationwide, even though healthcare professions are steadily increasing based on the baby boomers and an aging populations, the amount of AT graduates with a bachelor degree from the 300-plus accredited athletic training programs who are finding full-time employment upon graduation is around 50%. Unofficial tracking of those who aren't selected for athletic training positions are either pursuing another kinesiology career or attempting to qualify for a graduate program to strengthen their chances of becoming an athletic trainer by obtaining better credentials and/or experience through a graduate curriculum. Based on the latest information through the National Athletic Training Association (NATA), over 70% of currently employed athletic trainers possess either a master's or doctorate degree in a related field of kinesiology. This trend will not be promising to those athletic training students who are planning to seek open employment after completing a bachelor's degree program and passing the Board of Certification (BOC) for athletic training licensing.

Figure 5.1:

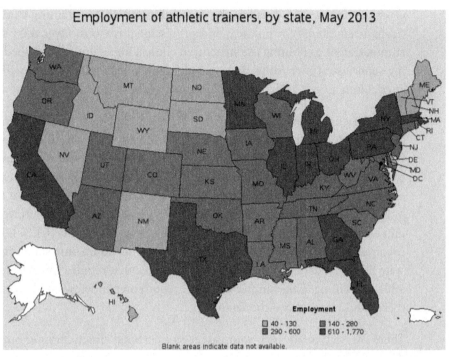

Source: http://www.bls.gov

Figure 5.2:

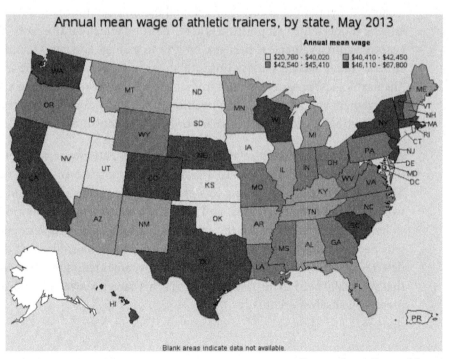

Source: http://www.bls.gov

Training, CEUs, Degree, License, Advancement Education Requirements

Over the past several decades, the curriculum of athletic training students has drastically been altered for political and professional reasons. Over the past decade, the elimination of combining the structured clinical hours under a certified athletic training supervisor (internships that ranged from 1,000 to 2,000 hours) with a formalized curriculum as well as the practical exams have resulted in mixed reviews.

Now, the current standard of being able to sit and take the BOC exam requires a bachelor's degree from a Commission on Accreditation in Allied Health Education Programs (CAAHEP) institution in athletic training. These would include specific coursework suitable to prepare a student to eventually sit for the BOC exam. The BOC exam consists of written questions and practical scenarios which are taken through online methods. Once you have successfully passed this BOC exam, you must maintain a code of ethics and provide Continuing Education Units (CEUs). Fifty CEUs are required every two years to maintain your certification. Some states do not require a state license. Currently, there are only 48 states that require this besides the BOC in athletic training. Checking select state requirements before applying for a position there would be the wise choice to make.

There are ways to advance your career as a certified athletic trainer but for many undergraduate students in kinesiology, sometimes thinking about the future is not a common theme. As we discussed in earlier chapters, it is important to take the time to forecast where your career should be in the next 5, 10, and 20-plus years (refer to Chapter 3/Pyramid of Success lab). Not all the time but for many entry-level certified athletic trainers, the first position is at an assistant athletic trainer job. Within several years of gaining valuable experience on how to manage and run a facility, the assistant athletic trainer usually parlays this into an associate or head athletic trainer position. The next logical progression after this step would be more toward an athletic or sport management and administration position, if the individual decided that this was the best direction to take for either salary or benefits acquisition.

Anecdotally, when asking several athletic trainers nationwide why they would leave this profession and move toward a management spot, the answer is very consistent. The burnout rate is high among this profession, especially after five to seven years of working 50-plus hours, nights, and weekends for athletic competitions. The ability to have set hours and reduce the amount of stress has been documented as reasons why people would leave this profession. Those who are raising young children can be deterred to other professions if childrearing becomes an issue. It is without question that you really need to be passionate about this career to overcome obstacles that will present themselves eventually.

Organization/Professional Memberships

NATA – National Athletic Trainers' Association. The NATA has over 35,000 members and has been around since 1950. For more information about careers in athletic training, contact:

National Athletic Trainers' Association
2952 Stemmons Freeway, Suite 200
Dallas, TX 75247
(214) 637-6282
www.nata.org

For more information about athletic trainer certification, contact:

Board of Certification, Inc.
4223 S. 143rd Circle
Omaha, NE 68137
(402) 559-0091
www.bocatc.org

Physical Therapy

The profession of physical therapy has been around since the beginning of World War I based on the need to rehabilitate our injured soldiers from battle. The onslaught of polio also played a vital role with training specialists to assist with mobility and improve movement function due to the impairments of this disease. Under the auspices of the American Medical Association until the 1950s, the American Physical Therapy Association (APTA) was created to ensure proper licensure and board certification across the country. Today, physical therapists are medically trained and licensed healthcare professionals who provide care and treatment to all age groups with regards to physical functioning.

What Do Physical Therapists Do?

Physical therapists treat people of all age groups who have movement problems. Many of these issues are based from an injury to post-surgery limitations. Common ailments are musculoskeletal such as lower back strains but also could be other joints within the body due to a broken bone or a pinched nerve. The ability to regain full range of motion and relieve pain is comforting and rewarding for these professionals and highly appreciative of those receiving these benefits. Physical therapists are trained to use a variety of methods to care for their patients or assigned individuals. These modalities are specific techniques used to treat their ailment and reduce the onset or continuous pain symptoms. Such treatments could be using cryotherapy, heat, electrical muscle stimulation, massage, ultrasound, or pressure upon the joints or connective tissues to enhance range of motion or stimulate the healing process of metabolism.

These days, many newly graduated and licensed physical therapists are acquiring more specific medical specialties, developed through more clinical rotations, research, and updated coursework in their graduate programs. Such specialties are in the areas of pediatrics, geriatrics, musculoskeletal, special populations such as developmental movement disorders, and rehabilitation of stroke or cardiac issues. Others are becoming more involved with athletic improvements through obtaining certifications in strength and conditioning and working with athletes of all levels in preparation of the sport besides the treatment of injuries.

Important Qualities for Physical Therapists

According to the Bureau of Labor Statistics, U.S. Department of Labor, Occupational Outlook Handbook, 2014-15 Edition, physical therapists are recommended to possess the following characteristics in order for them to be highly successful in this career field:

1. *Compassion.* Physical therapists are often drawn to this career in part by a desire to help people. Sometimes, it's based on a personal experience they had in their past. Their clients most likely will have pain symptoms and possessing empathy is acknowledged.
2. *Detail oriented.* Physical therapists should have an aptitude to diagnose a patient's problem, evaluate treatments, and provide sound treatment in order to make corrective solutions based on their observations and analytic skills.
3. *Dexterity.* Physical therapists use their hands constantly to provide therapy and assist with therapeutic exercises manually. This ability is a must in order to effectively massage or work on patients.
4. *Interpersonal skills.* Physical therapists must be able to communicate with patients with regards to treatment or intervention programs. The added ability to motivate patients, and listen to patients' needs will be appreciated and expected.
5. *Physical stamina.* Physical therapists provide a lot of manual labor through their modalities and techniques. This will require the ability to stand for long periods of time and create physical stress on the provider.
6. *Resourcefulness.* Physical therapists also provide additional resources to treat and educate patients. Being able to have other resources or skills such as athletic preparation or provide additional networking such as support groups can create a well-rounded healthcare provider.

Work Environment for Physical Therapists

There was over 195,000 employed physical therapists in the United States according to the Labor of Statistics May 2013 Report. Most physical therapists work in clinics, hospitals, assisted care centers, convalescent homes, and sport performance centers. The majority of them (55%) worked in physical therapy clinics or hospitals.

As stated earlier in the chapter, physical therapists spend a lot of time on their feet, physically working directly with patients. Due to the physicality of the work environment, these healthcare providers are also prone to obtaining physical injuries on the job. Physical therapists can reduce their risks of getting injured on the job by practicing proper body mechanics and lifting techniques when performing their scheduled duties on patients or clients. Also, staying physically active and maintaining a fit lifestyle can add protection by improving one's own personal strength and endurance capacities.

Employment Outlook for Physical Therapists

If you observe the United States Bureau of Labor Statistics (BLS), employment is steady among this career during the past several years. As of May 2013, public or private clinics provided the most employment for this career (36%), followed by general medical centers or hospitals (25%). The average mean annual salary was stated at $82,180 per year. The lowest 10th percentile was hovering around $56,000, while the 90th percentile of top wages was $113,300 per year. This did not include any extra hourly or per diem work performed after hours or on weekends and holidays. By observing Figures 5.3 and 5.4, you will notice the higher salaries in certain states in this country. Of course, the cost of living would play a role with the demographics and pay scale. Metropolitan or urban cities would have higher availability and more pay, both in annual salary and hourly rates compared to the rural towns or less populated areas. This would be true for most kinesiology-related professions, regardless.

The need for future physical therapists is predicted to improve to 36% from 2012 to 2022, much faster than the average of similar professions. This is most likely due to the aging baby boomers, since they are living longer and making better retirement plans including medical services. The aging population has significantly increased over the past several decades and this trend will not slow down in the near future. This specific population will require the services of physical therapists in many areas of practice. From pain relief to functional mobility to heart and lung ailments, their services will be in great demand.

In addition, patients with other chronic conditions such as diabetes, arthritis, and hypertension are increasing. More physical therapists are needed to help these patients maintain their functionality and manage the effects of these diseases. Advances in the medical field such as surgical procedures will create more need for physical therapists in postoperative care and rehabilitation.

According to unnamed physical therapy higher education sources, the passing rate for many accredited programs are close or higher to 90%, once you are able to gain entrance into an accredited master's or doctoral level PT program in the United States. The less than 10% who do not complete their studies or pass the National Board exams do end up in the healthcare field but not as physical therapists. Such need can be utilized in teaching at community colleges or universities who support PT assistant programs. Overall, it is a positive sign that such a high passing rate assures most students who can qualify into a program that their success at obtaining a job in physical therapy is very high.

Training, CEUs, Degree, License, Advancement Education Requirements

In 2013, there were 218 physical therapy programs nationwide accredited by the Commission on Accreditation in Physical Therapy Education, all of which offered either a master's degree (MPT) or the doctor of physical therapy (DPT) degree. DPT programs are three-year programs, including a research-intensive component during the third year. All PT programs require a bachelor's degree for admission as well as specific prerequisites, such as statistics, lifespan courses, and two complete semesters of the following courses: anatomy, physiology, biology, chemistry, and physics.

The graduate curriculum often includes courses in motion analysis, biomechanics, anatomy, physiology, neuroscience, and pharmacology. Clinical internships are performed during the third year, during which they gain supervised experience in specific areas of specialty such as neuromuscular or pediatrics. Physical therapists can apply to gain entrance towards a clinical residency program after graduating from their PT program. Residencies are about one year and provide additional training and experience in specialty areas of care.

All states require licensing by physical therapists. Licensing requirements are different in each state but all physical therapists must show proof of passing the National Physical Therapy Examination administered by the Federation of State Boards of Physical Therapy. Continuing Education Units (CEUs) are typically required for physical therapists maintaining their credentials. Each state has different requirements for obtaining and earning CEUs during either a calendar or biannual year.

Becoming a board-certified specialist can be a goal after working as a licensed physical therapist for several years post-graduate. Board specialist certification requires taking and passing an exam in the area of specialty. Also, a minimum of 2,000 hours of clinical work must be completed from an APTA-accredited residency program in that specialty area.

Figure 5.3:

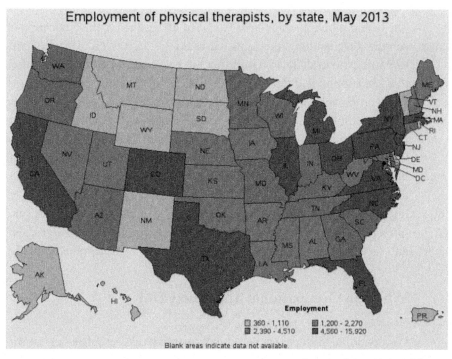

Source: http://www.bls.gov

Figure 5.4:

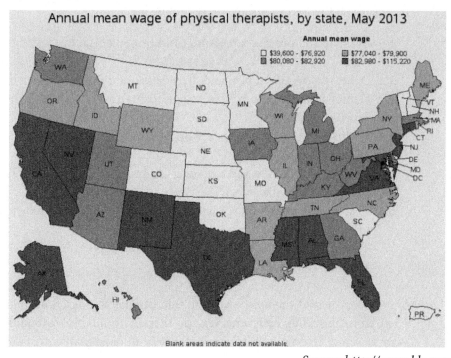

Source: http://www.bls.gov

Occupational Therapy

The occupational therapy field has been around since the beginning of the twentieth century. Occupational therapy focuses on the desires and wishes of patients who want to participate in daily activities that are considered meaningful to them. Notice how this philosophy is different from the field of physical therapy even though there is some crossover with regard to returning someone to a functional sense, regardless of the technique or treatment. If certain skills or tasks are unable to be completed or accomplished by the patient, the occupational therapist finds agreeable solutions to these challenges in order to create a functioning daily lifestyle for the client, including both children and adults. The main organization known as the American Occupational Therapy Association (AOTA) was established in 1917 to represent the interests, integrity of the career, and future concerns of occupational therapists and OT students. The organization is responsible for licensing, providing resources, setting standards, and serving as representative toward improving healthcare nationwide.

What Do Occupational Therapists Do?

Occupational therapists treat patients as physical therapists do, but through the therapeutic use of daily activities. They help people complete tasks for daily living and working activities through useful therapeutic techniques vs. more standard modalities that PT practitioners would prescribe. According to the Board of Labor Statistics, occupational therapists typically do the following:

1. Evaluate and observe a patient's condition, medical history, ability to perform tasks
2. Develop a treatment plan and provide specific goals to be accomplished
3. Demonstrate specific exercises to perform to assist with relieving pain and improving performance
4. Evaluate the client's home or work station and identify potential hazards and assist with improvements
5. Educate their family and employer about their condition and how to support future implications
6. Recommend the use of special equipment, if needed, and how to operate these tools
7. Test, record, and reassess for progress and report this to their physician or healthcare provider

Some occupational therapists work in educational settings, working with disabled children or providing early intervention therapy to infants or toddlers. Others will work in senior settings, such as assisted care or nursing homes, to assess patients and help with their living or working environments. Occupational therapists also may work in mental health settings or may work with individuals who have problems with chemical dependency issues or other mental health disorders. Those who suffer from stress or stress-related disorders may also be treated by occupational therapists.

Important Qualities of an Occupational Therapist

According to the Bureau of Labor Statistics, U.S. Department of Labor, Occupational Outlook Handbook, 2014-15 Edition, occupational therapists are recommended to possess the following characteristics in order for them to be highly successful in this career field:

1. **Communication skills.** Occupational therapists should have the skills to listen attentively to what patients tell them and be able discuss the plan to improve their current conditions.
2. **Compassion.** Occupational therapists are empathetic towards the needs of their patients and want to help in any way possible to improve their current conditions.
3. **Flexibility.** Occupational therapists must be creative and have the ability to attempt new techniques or methods if current agenda are not effective.
4. **Interpersonal skills.** Occupational therapists should be able to earn the trust and respect of their patients through their honesty, interactions, and consistent positive behaviors.
5. **Patience.** Occupational therapists should understand that patients will be frustrated with slow progress. This virtue is important to demonstrate with all clients and patients to keep them calm and promote continued support.
6. **Writing skills.** When providing feedback to the medical team or physician, good report writing and grammar demonstrates professionalism and respect among peers and colleagues.

Work Environment for Occupational Therapists

According the Bureau of Labor Statistics Report of 2013, occupational therapists held about 113,200 jobs in 2012. The industries that employed the most occupational therapists in 2012 are as listed below:

Hospitals: state, local, and private - 28%; Offices of physical, occupational and speech therapists, and audiologists – 22%; Elementary and secondary schools: state, local, and private - 12%; Nursing care facilities – 9%; and Home healthcare services – 9%. Occupational therapists spend a lot of time on their feet while working with a variety of clients, both young or elderly. Physical tasks such as lifting heavy equipment and moving patients will be necessary. Staying physically active and maintaining a fit lifestyle can add protection by improving one's own personal strength and endurance capacities. Traveling to different work or job sites is common among this profession and per diem work is also a possibility.

Employment Outlook for Occupational Therapists

If you observe the United States Bureau of Labor Statistics (BLS), employment is steady among this career during the past several years. There are over 108,000 licensed occupational therapists employed in the United States as of May 2013. The mean average salary nationwide is currently $77,790 annually (Figures 5.5 and 5.6). Employment of occupational therapists is projected to grow 29% from 2012 to 2022, based on the increase of clients due to the baby boom generation and people who are living longer. The lower end of the salary scale for occupational therapists is $51,310 (10th percentile) while the higher range at the 90th percentile is $109,380 per year. This annual base salary is dependent upon the demographics, needs, and availability of licensed occupational therapists within the boundaries of the United States. Demand for these services is based on the ability of patients to pay, either directly or through some form of health insurance. Services in this career field may increase because of federal health insurance reforms and federal mandates to provide everyone with a form of health insurance. Both rehabilitation and similar services are considered essential health benefits that insurers will need to cover once these reforms are approved by the federal government.

Training, CEUs, Degree, License, Advancement Education Requirements

Occupational therapists need a minimum of a master's degree in occupational therapy, even though discussions are ongoing with accreditation to require OTs to possess a doctoral degree. As expected with their counterparts in physical therapy, OTs must be licensed or registered in the state they choose to work for. As of March 2013, there were 149 occupational therapy programs accredited by the Accreditation Council for Occupational Therapy Education. Of the 149 accredited programs in the United States, only 145 are master's degree and 4 are doctoral degree programs.

Admission to graduate programs in occupational therapy generally requires a bachelor's degree and specific coursework, very similar to PT entrance requirements. Many of these graduate programs require students to have volunteered or worked in an OT worksite. Master's degree programs take two to three years to complete while the doctoral programs take about three years. Some schools offer a dual-degree program in which the student earns a bachelor's degree and a master's degree in five years. Part-time programs exist at some institutions that offer courses during evenings and weekends The master's and doctoral degree programs require a minimum of 24 weeks of supervised fieldwork, resulting in these prospective occupational therapists gaining clinical work experience.

Figure 5.5:

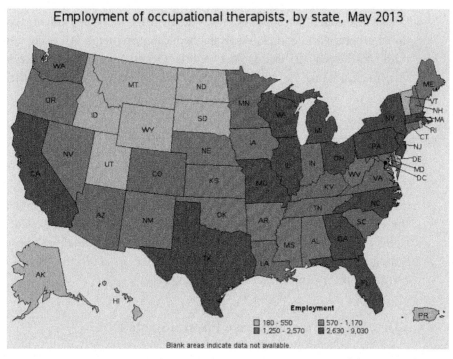

Source: http://www.bls.gov

Figure 5.6:

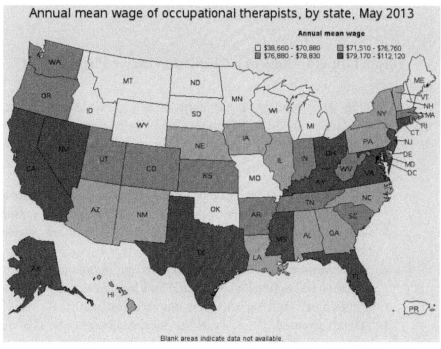

Source: http://www.bls.gov

All states require occupational therapists to pass the national examination administered by the National Board for Certification in Occupational Therapists (NBCOT). In order to take this exam, the candidates must have earned a degree from an accredited educational program and completed all fieldwork requirements. All occupational therapists must pass the NBCOT exam to use the title "Occupational Therapist Registered" (OTR). They must also take Continuing Education Units (CEUs) to maintain their certification.

Clinical Exercise Physiologist

The term "exercise physiologist" has been around since the early 1970s, most likely derived by the combination of using cardiac rehabilitation and clinical fitness testing on high-risk patients. The American Physiological Society recognized this term in the 1970s as a specialty area to the discipline of physiology. By 1974, the American College of Sports Medicine (ACSM) developed specific guidelines to promote exercise testing and prescription at hospitals and clinics. In 2000, the ACSM developed the certification for clinical exercise physiologists.

What Do Clinical Exercise Physiologists Do?

Exercise physiologists apply the principles of exercise physiology to develop fitness and exercise programs that help patients prevent, reduce, or recover from chronic illnesses and improve cardiovascular function, body composition, strength, muscular endurance, and overall flexibility.

Important Qualities of a Clinical Exercise Physiologist

According to the Bureau of Labor Statistics, U.S. Department of Labor, Occupational Outlook Handbook, 2014-15 Edition, clinical exercise physiologists are recommended to possess the following characteristics in order for them to be highly successful in this career field.

1. **Compassion.** Clinical exercise physiologists work with clients who may be patients, athletes, or general population, suffering from considerable pain or discomfort. They must be sympathetic while providing assessments, exercise prescriptions, and follow-up appointments.
2. **Decision-making skills.** Clinical exercise physiologists must be able to make decisions regarding how much and how long an assessment or test should continue, based on the participant's physiological results.
3. **Detail oriented.** Clinical exercise physiologists must be able to create and provide detailed, accurate information about their patients or clients who are receiving the appropriate assessments, treatments, or prescribed fitness routines.

4. **Interpersonal skills.** Clinical exercise physiologists must have strong interpersonal communication skills to relate well with others. This includes physicians, patients, athletes, coaches, and parents.

Work Environment for Clinical Exercise Physiologists

Clinical exercise physiologists work in hospitals, outpatient clinics, wellness centers, and sport enhancement facilities. According to the Board of Labor Statistics, the industries that employed the most clinical exercise physiologists in 2012 are listed below:

Medical outpatients and surgical hospitals - 53%; Ambulatory healthcare facilities – 21%; Specialty hospitals focusing on cardiovascular care – 6%; and Nursing and residential care facilities – 4%. Most clinical exercise physiologists work full time during normal business hours. About 33% work part time while having other kinesiology-related employment opportunities to supplement their income.

Employment Outlook for Exercise Physiologists

Employment of clinical exercise physiologists is projected to grow 9% from 2012 to 2022 according to the Board of Labor Statistics Annual Report May 2013, based on the forecasting of similar related professions. This is a much smaller occupation field and compared to athletic trainers, licensure for clinical exercise physiologists is less common and therefore there are fewer opportunities for national recognition for this occupation. Demand may rise as hospitals emphasize exercise and preventive care as part of their treatment for chronic diseases and long-term rehabilitation. There are always available clinical exercise physiologist positions in larger metropolitan areas (Figures 5.7 and 5.8); however, the field is very competitive among recent college graduates. The median annual wage for clinical exercise physiologists was $44,770 in May 2012. The lowest 10% earned less than $31,000, and the top 10% earned more than $70,140 annually.

Training, CEUs, Degree, License, Advancement Education Requirements

Clinical exercise physiologists need a minimum of a bachelor's degree from an accredited college or university. Master's degrees are the preferred level for many clinical positions nationwide. Both degree programs have classroom and clinical components, including science and health-related courses, such as biology, anatomy, physiology, biomechanics, test and prescription, including nutrition. The Committee on Accreditation for the Exercise Sciences is a national organization that overseas many exercise physiology programs.

Just a few states require clinical exercise physiologists to be licensed although more states are proactively seeking new legislation to institute license requirements. The American Society of Exercise Physiologists (ASEP) offers the Clinical Exercise Physiologist Certified (EPC) certification that physiologists can advertise and display to legitimize their profession and credentials. The EPC requires formal completion of a kinesiology-related bachelor's degree program, completing the ASEP exam, and taking Continuing Education Units (CEUs) every three to five years to maintain the certification. The American College of Sports Medicine (ACSM) also offers several different certifications for clinical exercise physiologists. The Certified Clinical Exercise Specialist (CES) certifications are for candidates with only bachelor's degrees in a kinesiology-related field and the Registered Clinical Exercise Physiologist (RCEP) certificates are for those practitioners holding master's degrees or higher. Clinical exercise physiologists often will have additional opportunities to advance into management positions after serving in their prospective positions for several years and gaining more insight into the operational day-to-day activities that would be necessary to advance to this supervisory area of facility management.

Figure 5.7:

Source: http://www.bls.gov

Figure 5.8:

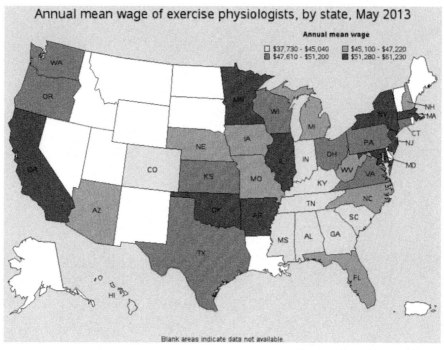

Source: http://www.bls.gov

CHAPTER 6

Coaching Professions in Sport or Sport Instruction

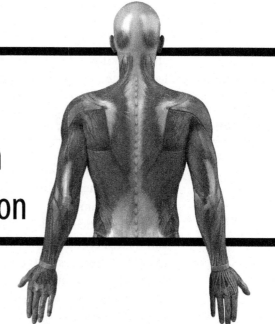

The concept of "coaching" is extremely vague these days since everyone does some aspect or confirms to a style of leadership towards directing a team or a set of individuals. Perhaps, it won't be exactly the same premise but for the sake of seeking and obtaining a good career, let's focus on the true nature of what the profession of coaching is and what makes a successful coaching career that kinesiology majors can consider.

Coaches instruct, direct, and produce results from athletes in team or individual sports. In individual sports, a coach can be a teaching instructor. The duties of a coach or sport instructor can be related as well as different. Both entities train athletes for competition through practice sessions, work on improving sport biomechanics, and focus on strength and conditioning. Both evaluate the athletes and develop strategies against their opponents. However, there are times where coaches are not allowed to instruct their athletes during competition. Leading an individual or team to a successful result is extremely rewarding regardless if you consider yourself a coach or a sport instructor. For the sake of keeping consistency with the chapter itself, I will group both terms together as one profession to diffuse any confusion about this career path.

Former athletes also want to continue their successful or winning ways from the past. Coaching a sport or an individual activity allows this to continue if you have this passion to improve or lead athletes in the sport. However, the philosophy of winning at any or all costs won't play a role towards your decision to pursue this profession since not all of us will be able to win all the time and it sends the wrong message to those you intend to coach about what sport participation really represents. Let's talk about the levels of coaching you intend to reach for without losing perspective towards what success really is in this profession. Coaches can work and teach amateur and professional athletes the skills they need to become successful in their selected activity. A

Scout is a "coach" who observes for new and upcoming athletes, evaluating potential athletic skills and projecting likelihood for success at the next level—that is, the college, amateur, or professional level.

What Is the Profession of Coaching?

The profession of a "coach" will strictly focus on being fully employed at a level where kinesiology majors can be pursuing this profession by completing their undergraduate degree program. Yes, there are coaching positions that are volunteer or part time, but for the sake of enticing full-time career opportunities, this chapter will focus on the relevant careers that are obtainable. This chapter will not focus on the professional levels where those opportunities will be very few and minimal to most people who do pursue this occupation. Of course, if it is your life-seeking goal to obtain this level of achievement, by no means am I discouraging you from this. It's just unlikely for most kinesiology majors to be the head coach of the Los Angeles Lakers compared to seeking a head coach position at the regional university or college level. I believe the latest statistics show that less than 1% of those in the coaching profession will obtain the head coach position of a major professional organization. Based on these statistics, I will encourage you to be more realistic and seek those coaching positions that will be obtainable in your lifetime.

Important Qualities of a Coach

According to the Bureau of Labor Statistics, U.S. Department of Labor, Occupational Outlook Handbook, 2014-15 Edition, all coaches are recommended to possess the following characteristics in order for them to be highly successful in this career field.

1. **Communication skills.** Coaches provide instruction and organization, and motivate athletes so they must develop excellent communication skills. Effective communication will ensure proper techniques, strategies, and rules of the sport so all participants will fully comprehend the information provided.
2. **Decision-making skills.** Coaches must select the best players to use at a given position during the game and seek a strategy that results in the best chance for winning. Coaches and scouts also must be very selective when recruiting players that demonstrate potential at the next level of instruction.
3. **Dedication.** Coaches must be physically available during practices and facilitate the individual athletes in improving physical skills and mental conditioning. Coaches must understand that this trait takes years to develop in order to become successful.
4. **Interpersonal skills**. Coaches should be able to relate well to others in order to foster positive relationships and recruit potential players by developing this important characteristic.

5. **Leadership skills.** Coaches must have good leadership skills to motivate and push athletes. They must be leaders both on and off the playing field.
6. **Resourcefulness.** Coaches must take all available facets of the skills listed above to achieve the best chances for winning.

Work Environments for Potential Coaches

According to the Bureau of Labor Statistics, coaches and scouts held 243,900 jobs during 2012 while 11% were self-employed. The facilities that employed coaches and scouts during 2012 were the following: Elementary and secondary schools – 25%; Colleges, universities, or professional schools – 19%; Other private schools and instructional facilities – 17%; Amusement and recreation industries – 15%; and Civic or professional organizations – 5%. The typical work environment may be both indoors and outdoors, depending upon the type of sport or activity and could be year-round if weather plays a role when an activity of sport season begins or ends. Coaches often work nontraditional hours, including evenings, weekends, and holidays. They usually exceed 40 hours a week during the sport's season, if not annually. Some coaches will work part time, and may coach several sports during the year.

Employment Outlook for Coaches

The employment of coaches is projected to grow around 15% during the next decade, faster than similar occupations in the kinesiology field (Figure 6.1). Increasing participation in secondary schools and college sports could increase the need for coaches. Student athletics in high schools all across this country are projected to increase during the next 10 years. As a result of this trend, secondary schools may offer more sport programs which in turn allow college sports to feed into this growth, particularly at smaller colleges and in women's sports. Many smaller colleges that weren't offering athletic programs are now willing to increase the numbers especially at the Division III arena since athletic scholarships are not offered at this level.

This trend at both the secondary schools and college level could facilitate the involvement in professional sports hiring more coaches. Demonstrating success through a particular athletic program could foster more interest in certain institutions based on their reputation. This in turn could increase future student enrollment and allow larger donations from alumni. Four-year institutions will need to rely on the coaching staff to recruit talented high school athletes. Furthermore, as higher education tuition increases and scholarships become more coveted, the parents of promising high school athletes will hire coaches who can increase their child's chances of getting a partial or full ride opportunity at a four-year school.

Figure 6.1:

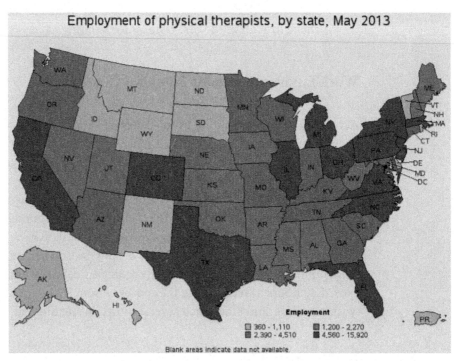

Source: http://www.bls.gov

Training, CEUs, Degree, License, Advancement Education Requirements

Coaches will need a bachelor's degree for the majority of coaching positions unless they are seeking private employment through a club or sport facility. It is also expected that their knowledge of the sport is very extensive. Not always, but many coaches usually obtain their knowledge through their own experiences of playing the sport at a very competitive level. Although past experience may be helpful, it is not required for some coaching positions if the person is motivated to learn or obtain experience through clinics or mentoring. For example, secondary schools usually hire licensed teachers who work there to perform the coaching duties. If a teacher is not available or has the background to coach a particular sport, the athletic director or principal of the school could hire a qualified candidate from the outside. Most state high school athletic associations require coaches to have a certification. Certification often requires coaches to be of a minimum age (at least 18 years old) and possess a valid cardiopulmonary resuscitation (CPR) and first-aid card from an approved vendor. Check to see if your state requires coaches to attend classes related to sports safety and coaching fundamentals prior to becoming certified. Although most public high school coaches need to meet these requirements, a certification may not be required for coaches or instructors at private or parochial schools. For more information on education requirements for teachers, see Chapter 7 in this text.

College level and professional sport coaches must have at least a bachelor's degree from an accredited institution. The four-year degree can be from any subject but many coaches do select a kinesiology-related degree in case the job entails that they also provide instruction to students in an exercise-related topic. College and professional coaching jobs also require player experience in that particular activity or sport at a competitive level. Additional certification may be highly desirable or even required in certain sports or activities. There are many certifying organizations specific to the various sports, and their requirements vary.

Many coaches begin their careers as assistant coaches to gain the knowledge and experience needed to become a head coach. Large schools and colleges that compete at the highest levels require a head coach with substantial experience at another school or as an assistant coach. To reach the ranks in the professional level, a candidate will need several years of coaching experience and a successful record at the lower ranks before any consideration is given. Networking was discussed in Chapters 3 and 4. Refer to these helpful tips in order to work your way up your Pyramid of Career Success.

Junior to Senior High School Assistant and Head Coaches

Secondary schools follow the progression after elementary schools, most evolving after the sixth grade, but other school systems that have middle schools instead of junior highs can start students in the fifth grade, depending upon the school district layout. There isn't much need for assistant or head coaches at the primary level based on developmental motor skill enhancement being of priority over athletic competition, but there could be some exceptions nationwide, especially at private or club institutions who could afford these salaries. The secondary school systems often hire assistant and head coaches to facilitate their year-round sports programs as would private and club sport venues such as private tennis academies that are considered year round in Florida. Since these privately funded coaching jobs are very limited and do not require a college education, this section will strictly focus on the goal of using the kinesiology degree to obtain this profession.

What Do Secondary Schools Assistant and Head Coaches Do?

The assistant coach will work under the direction of the head coach and athletic administrator to prepare the student athletes adequately for participation. Such participation would include practicing drills; game preparation; checking out equipment and uniforms; working with teachers, staff members, and parents to disseminate practice and game information and scheduling; tracking important practice and game statistics; and leading the team in the absence of the head coach. The head coach would work under the direction of the athletic director and/or principal of the school or the school superintendent. The duties of the head coach are similar to those of the assistant coach with the exception of this role being more in a leadership position as well as being the spokesperson for the team. Head coaches would have total authoritative power over the assistant coaches in many instances.

Each individual school district has strict salary guidelines for paying assistant and head coaches. There are school districts that do not provide for full- or part-time paid positions based on the school district's policies towards afterschool programs. So be prepared to either become an unpaid volunteer or receive a small stipend for your contributions when you first begin your coaching career. The salary for secondary level assistant coaches varies widely based on the financial well-being of the school district and policies established by state government, sport administrators of the state, or state high school athletic associations. There are some school districts that have a policy that requires all head and assistant coaches to work in some full-time capacity within the school or school district. Many coaches do teach full-time for either the school or school district while earning a teaching salary (which will be covered in another chapter in this text). Salaries as a teacher in the school provide the ability to contribute to volunteer coaching duties for some employees, depending upon their seniority and placement, and degree credits status.

Other school districts will provide another form of pay called a stipend to secondary school coaches. Stipends are money paid either monthly in a lump sum at the end of the season or completed contractual period. The head coach usually receives the largest stipends compared to the assistant coaches. An average stipend for an assistant coach is in the range of $1,000 to $5,000, depending on the policies determined by the individual school or school district. Sometimes the popular sports, such as basketball and football, will receive more stipend money than less attended ones. Some school districts use sliding scales to award larger stipends to assistant coaches with years of experience. Years of experience, type of college degree, any additional certifications such as coaching minors, etc. all provide the ability to increase one's stipend over the next several years for either the assistant or head coach.

There will be certain schools in this country that will pay assistant and head coaches a full-time annual salary. These salaries range in the ballpark of $20,000 to $50,000 per year. High schools that pay salaries to assistant and head coaches tend to feature a common characteristic. Private or charter schools provide these salaries based on the popular sports of football, basketball, or baseball. These private schools tend to pay more to assistant or head coaches who have years of service to the school compared to those who are starting their first year at the institution.

Employment opportunities at the high school level are decent for entry-level and seasoned coaches, but coaching jobs typically favor faculty teaching at the school. Those who have a degree or are state-certified to teach academic subjects have the highest chances of securing a coaching position at high schools. The need to replace the coaches who leave or retire will provide more opportunities. Also, based on the support of Title IX, those candidates who can coach girls' and women's sports may have better job opportunities and face less opposition compared to coaching boys' or men's sports.

Qualifications for becoming an assistant or head coach including a bachelor's degree in a fitness- or kinesiology-related field are highly recommended but not always necessary. There are coaching positions open for anyone who has a background in the sport or the ability to organize a team within the state regulations. Having a history of successful stints as an athlete, coach, or leader of a sport organization becomes helpful. Most public schools will perform a criminal background check and ask for a current first aid, CPR, and/or AED card. Letters of reference demonstrating your ability to lead and coach effectively are also helpful toward obtaining a job in the secondary schools. The private or parochial schools will have more flexibility with salary and requirements compared to your public institutions.

Physical Education Teaching/Coaching Combination

Assistant and head athletic coaches nationwide do pursue a career as a health and physical education teacher as a path toward becoming an assistant or head coach at a secondary school system. Usually, the coaching assignments are for extra pay and/or stipend and performed along with the teaching contract. The candidate must typically earn a bachelor's degree in physical education or a kinesiology-related field. The coursework taken would consist of general education classes such as communications, history, liberal arts, natural science, college-level math, technology, and a foreign language. The physical education curriculum would have core health classes such as first aid, prevention and care of athletic injuries, exercise physiology, and biomechanics. The core physical education requirements would include teaching theory classes for athletic activities such as gymnastics, dance, individual and dual sports, and team sport theory instruction.

Those physical education students who want to coach at the secondary level would either minor in coaching or take several coaching classes to qualify for a state certification, if that particular state requires one (check your individual state to see if a valid coaching certification is needed). Those candidates who want to seek a minor in coaching or a coaching certification could take specific classes ranging from an introduction into coaching to two or three specific coaching sport theory courses, along with a three or four classes consisting of biomechanics, exercise physiology, first aid/CPR, and prevention of athletic injuries before one is qualified to apply for coaching positions in that particular state at the secondary level.

While in college, it would be highly recommended that the student get involved in intercollegiate or intramural sports. If not at the local level, coaching can be enhanced by participating in club sports as a volunteer coach. By participating in a particular sport or athletic activity early on, an aspiring assistant or head coach can gain an appreciation of the leadership, organization, strategies, and development of athletes. This also would be helpful toward introducing them to an experience that could lead into a lifetime profession. The future outlook for secondary school coaching is very good since retirements have been steady for the past several years. It is dependent upon the region of the country and the population of the region to determine the availability of openings and salary for this career.

Community College and Four-Year Institution Assistant and Head Coaches

There are thousands of public and private colleges or universities all across this country. Most of these places offer intercollegiate sports at different levels of competitiveness. The largest community college state is California with 109 compared to the State of South Dakota which has no community colleges but offers 10 private and public four-year institutions. All provide offerings of employment on a regular basis if you have the background and experience. Two-year community or junior colleges have different requirements than four-year institutions. The majority of community colleges do not hire full-time assistant or head coaches unless you have a teaching component to your contract. It is common for successful assistant or head high school coaches to transition to the community college or a four-year institution as long as they meet hiring requirements of that institution.

What Do Community College Assistant and Head Coaches Do?

For many two-year institutions of higher education, many will offer a split contract consisting of a 60% coaching assignment and a 40% teaching assignment. Your teaching assignment is based on your educational experience or degree you possess. Most coaches would have a kinesiology-based degree so teaching activity courses and theory is common as well as health or wellness lecture classes. As for coaching duties, the following duties are common among four-year institutions.

1. Assist with evaluating and recruiting of student-athletes to the community college.
2. Supervise in all areas of team management including pre-season, post-season training, practice and competition.
3. Facilitate specific position or individual events that are associated with the sport or activity.
4. Work closely with the athletic staff for athletic performance of the student-athletes and the development of academic success.
5. Assist with the supervision of strength and conditioning sessions.
6. Assist with the daily operations including but not limited to main athletic association's paperwork which includes: academic monitoring, travel plans, equipment and budget management.

7. Provide student-athletes with their academic, athletic, and personal development.
8. Represent the institution at local, state, and regional athletic venues or events.
9. Understand the concept of compliance with the athletic association's policies with institutional rules guidelines that govern the league or conference.

Two-Year Community or Junior College Training, CEUs, Educational Requirements to Coach

Every state community college system has different requirements toward becoming an assistant or head coach of a particular sport that is being offered at this two-year level. Some will require just a bachelor's degree in a kinesiology- or sport-related major. Other states will allow a bachelor's degree in any field of study just as long as the candidate has prior experience as an intercollegiate athlete and coaching experience at either the secondary level or at a similar level. Experience could be as a graduate assistant for a college athletic program during their graduate studies. Other states such as California will require a master's degree in kinesiology or a related field along with successful coaching experience at the secondary level or similarly at a two-year community or junior college institution.

What Do Four-Year University or College Assistant and Head Coaches Do?

Unlike their two-year community or junior college coach counterparts, the four-year university or collegiate coaches do not have a teaching assignment as part of their contract. They are expected to devote all their efforts full time toward the overall success of their athletic program. Possessing a kinesiology-related degree does not play a major factor toward hiring a full-time coach at this level. Here are their expected duties:

1. Assist with evaluating and recruiting of student-athletes from the high school to the two-year colleges towards matriculating into the four-year institution.
2. Supervise in all areas of team management including pre-season, post-season training, practice, and competition.
3. Facilitate specific position or individual events that are associated with the sport or activity.
4. Work closely with the athletic staff for athletic performance of the student-athletes and the development of academic success to maintain eligibility and promote graduation requirements.
5. Assist with the supervision of strength and conditioning sessions with the strength and conditioning staff at the college or university.

6. Assist with the daily operations including but not limited to main athletic association's paperwork (NCAA or NAIA) which includes: academic monitoring, travel plans, equipment and budget management.
7. Provide student-athletes with their academic, athletic, and personal development towards the community and institution.
8. Represent the institution at local, state, regional, and national athletic venues or events.
9. Understand the concept of compliance with the athletic association's policies with institutional rules and guidelines that govern the league or conference, may this be the NCAA or NAIA.
10. Hire and maintain supervision of other associate or assistant coaches who you would supervise.

Employment Outlook for Two- and Four-Year Assistant and Head College Coaches

The salary scale is considered a wide range because they are dependent on multiple factors, including the candidate's experience, the size of the university or college, and the team's record. As of May 2012, the U.S. Bureau of Labor Statistics reported a mean annual salary of $36,680 for all coaches. Head coaches of major sports will command a much higher salary compared to assistant coaches, with a median salary of $70,354 and the top 10% bringing in more than $110,000 annually as of November 2013. Competition will be very strong for the coveted top spots at the major institutions as there are very few positions available at these highly preferred positions for coaching opportunities. On a larger scale for assistant and head coaches, employment should experience a great deal of growth, with a 29% increase in jobs expected from 2010 to 2020, according to the Board of Labor Statistics if you include all two-year and four-year institutions nationwide.

The Strength and Conditioning Coach

Strength and conditioning coaches are not considered personal trainers or group exercise leaders even though they do help others improve their fitness levels. They are in a major leadership role, just like an assistant or head coach of a collegiate program. Another major difference between these professionals and personal trainers is, the philosophical work ethic is focused on improving performance or skill in a sport vs. just one's overall wellness. This is why strength and conditioning coaches work primarily with athletes. Strength and conditioning coaches have two primary goals. The first is to improve athletic performance, which usually means improving athletes' speed, strength, and power (although specifics vary according to athlete and sport). Conditioning coaches develop systematic training programs for both teams and individual athletes, often working in close association with coaches. This usually includes teaching proper lifting techniques, supervising and motivating athletes as they work out, and assessing their performance before and after the program. The nature of the conditioning program will vary depending on whether the sport is in season or not. During the off-season, conditioning programs can be quite rigorous. In season, conditioning programs tend to focus more on maintaining athletes' conditioning than on improving it. Conditioning programs also vary by sport, and even by position within the sport. The second goal is to create a winning program, sometimes at all costs. Job security can be based on wins and losses. When the team wins, the coaching staff usually stays intact. When the team loses, coaches are let go, including the strength and conditioning staff. It is a reality among the elites that this practice continues at all levels of athletics.

Historically, strength and conditioning coaches have been around since the 1970s, a period when a small group of powerlifting coaches, athletic coaches, and physical educators decided to create a strength and conditioning forum called the National Strength & Conditioning Association (NSCA). Strength coaches were not recognized as a profession back then. Mr. Bob Devaney, the head football coach and athletic director at the University of Nebraska decided to hire the very first strength and conditioning coach for an athletic program in the United States. That coach ended up being Mr. Boyd Epley, a former Nebraska record holder in the pole vault. After acknowledging the success Mr. Epley had with the Nebraska athletes, other schools across the country began to hire strength and conditioning coaches for their athletic programs.

According to the NSCA website, "The National Strength & Conditioning Association was founded in 1978 with 76 strength coaches from across the country with the common desire to network, collaborate and unify the profession of strength and conditioning. Since its inception, the NSCA has grown to nearly 30,000 members in 72 countries and become the leader in the research and education of strength and conditioning professionals." There are currently 37 provincial state directors for the NSCA and every state is required to host state clinics and conferences, along with a regional and national conference annually to promote and disseminate information and research in the areas of strength and conditioning. By the 1980s, the very first certification program was offered by the NSCA to certify strength and conditioning coaches as certified specialists known as the Certified Strength & Conditioning Specialist (CSCS), an elite standard held today to recognize those candidates who have the expertise to apply scientific knowledge and train athletes for the primary goal of improving athletic performance.

Job Duties of a Strength and Conditioning Coach

A strength and conditioning coach will coordinate with the head athletic coaches for each sport to provide a comprehensive year-round schedule for strength and conditioning workouts for each team or team member. In an ideal situation, college athletic departments will hire one strength and conditioning coach for every 10 to 20 athletes who use the athletic strength and conditioning facility. The actual number of such coaches is less than the ideal conditions, however. Depending on the size of the athletic program and the level of competition, there might be as few as one or two strength and conditioning coaches. An example of such staffing would be the University of Notre Dame. They have nine full-time strength and conditioning coaches who train 750 student-athletes compared to Central College in Pella, Iowa, which has two full-time strength and conditioning coaches who work with 450 student-athletes. At the professional ranks, you usually have more strength and conditioning coaches training with fewer athletes. For example, the Washington Redskins of the National Football League have three full-time strength and conditioning coaches for 70-plus football players compared to the San Antonio Spurs of the National Basketball Association who have one strength and conditioning coach for 15 basketball players.

The strength and conditioning coach provides expert instruction in the use of weight modalities and conditioning equipment or gear. Based on the needs of the athletic team or members, this input is highly important to create a complete program to follow from pre-season, in-season, to off-season cycling or periodization cycles. The strength and conditioning coach will also work with the staff to maintain the upkeep of the equipment, inventory of all issued gear and available gear, supervision of the facilities when being used by athletes, and tracking of all athletes in order to report their status to their respective sport coaches on a regular basis. The strength and conditioning coach will also work with the athletic training staff, especially if rehabilitation or specific conditioning of an athlete is warranted and feedback of the results of their workout program is warranted. Some organizations require the strength and conditioning coach to maintain the weight room(s) for both athletes and nonathletes. In this role, an inventory of equipment will be a necessity as well as suggesting upgrades to the existing equipment. Sometimes, the college or university will give authority to hire weight room staff supervisors, may they be student workers or graduate assistants. Also, acting as a liaison with the kinesiology or exercise science program, they should educate the athletes on strength and conditioning principles and current theories as well as provide educational resources on nutrition and supplements.

Important Qualities of a Secondary Assistant and Head Strength Coach

Supervising and directing strength and conditioning programs can be very rigorous and it can be challenging to train athletes at high levels of performance. For this reason, strength and conditioning coaches must be able to motivate constantly. Because of the diversity of student-athletes, strength and conditioning coaches must be organized, detail oriented, and good at multitasking. Much like a college professor, a strength and conditioning coach must educate student-athletes on how to properly train with weights and other exercises in order to improve their performance. Strength and conditioning coaches should be perceptive to the athletes' behaviors, watching the athletes during the training sessions, and making corrections to biomechanics or lifting protocols when needed. Finally, to work successfully not only with student-athletes, the strength and conditioning coach must have great interpersonal skills to communicate with other staff members, other coaches, administrators, professors, and parents, besides competing strength and conditioning staff from opposing programs.

Work Environments for Potential Strength and Conditioning Coaches

With the advancement of scientific research in strength and conditioning over the past several years, all such coaches must recognize utilizing more technology toward conditioning athletes, regardless of the age or type of facility or building. A strength and conditioning facility at most colleges or universities should resemble a weight room with simple office and administrative workstations, but having significantly more free weights and platforms than just machine weight equipment since strength and power are optimized to ensure greater success for the athletes. Also, more strength and conditioning coaches are being employed by secondary school districts, public or private fitness centers, physical therapy clinics, and professional athletic venues. Sport enhancement or performance centers are becoming popular nationwide, which opens up more opportunities for strength and conditioning coaches to work outside colleges and universities. Facilities would be newer and possess less space but functional. Facilities in this case do not need to be large and is likely to provide simple pieces of equipment toward improving agility, speed, and sport-specific performance for the general population.

Training, CEUs, Degree, License, Advancement Education Requirements

Most colleges and universities, including professional organizations, require strength and conditioning coaches to hold at minimum a bachelor's degree in kinesiology or a related field. However, the majority of job offerings for strength and conditioning prefer a master's degree in kinesiology or a related degree. A strength and conditioning coach should possess years of experience at a facility or institution where strength and conditioning was the main focus. For those undergraduates who will be pursuing this career line, obtaining a proper internship at an established strength and conditioning program is essential. Experience might be equally as important in preparation for a career as a conditioning coach. The wise student will gain firsthand experience in strength and conditioning environments while still in college. Whether working as an assistant, an intern, or a volunteer, nothing is more important than gaining firsthand experience. Working in a fitness center is helpful in this regard, but most fitness centers are committed to improving health and fitness rather than athletic performance.

For this reason, it is also important to merge studies in kinesiology with experience working under the supervision, or mentoring, of a skilled strength and conditioning coach.

Fortunately many coaches like to share their expertise with enthusiastic young people interested in pursuing similar careers. As is true for the other fitness careers discussed in this chapter, it is worthwhile to become a member of a professional organization. The premier organization for strength and conditioning coaches is the National Strength & Conditioning Association (NSCA). Members have access to several journals focusing on the science behind conditioning as well as practical methods of doing so. It doesn't necessarily need to be at a college or university but should be supervised by a known strength and conditioning professional who has college and university relationships. Professional sport teams typically require the job candidate to demonstrate successful strength and conditioning experience at the university level for several years. High schools standards for strength and conditioning coaches are not as stringent but should demonstrate strength training experience working with minors.

Depending on the college athletic division or professional affiliates, a strength and conditioning coach will be required to obtain a professional certification in the field. Common certifications include those offered by the National Strength & Conditioning Association (NSCA) or the Collegiate Strength and Conditioning Coaches Association (CSCCA). The certifications between these two have commonalities. Both require the job candidate to have a bachelor's degree in kinesiology or a related field and pass the certification exam.

By August 2015, all strength and conditioning coaches who are seeking jobs at four-year schools whose athletic affiliations are with the National Collegiate Athletic Association (NCAA) not only must be familiar with NCAA rules and regulations, they must possess a Certified Strength & Conditioning Specialist (CSCS) certification. They must understand common medical terminology and have an operational knowledge of fitness and strength equipment. To work as a high school strength and conditioning coach, most school districts require a valid teaching licensure in the residing state or a valid substitute teaching license. A criminal background check will be conducted at all levels.

Employment Outlook for Strength and Conditioning Coaches

The job outlook for strength and conditioning coaches is very good based on the demographics of the United States (Figure 6.2). The competition for these jobs will be high, especially at the college and professional levels. Strong networking occurs among strength and conditioning circles at the regional or national conferences. It is common for strength and conditioning coaches to hire their assistants who have lineage from well-known strength coaches or programs. Establishing connections early (see Chapters 2 and 3 in this text) through mentoring and qualifying for competitive internships with nationally renowned strength and conditioning coaches are key to early success. If you need to qualify who the "movers and shakers" are in this industry, go to the regional or national conferences and you will know who they are, once you have attended the week-long programs. You will find strength and conditioning coaches who are employed at the private or corporate levels which may interest you more so than pursuing just colleges and universities for a job. In a recent survey performed by the American College of Sports Medicine (ACSM), strength and conditioning coaching was one of the top five employment trends this past year. Based on these findings, this career does have major potential for kinesiology students to pursue this for the next several years.

Figure 6.2:

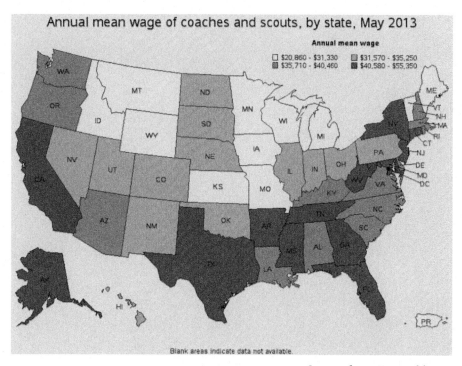

Source: *http://www.bls.gov*

Salaries for strength and conditioning coaches vary, depending upon the education background, experience, and certifications. The average salary is between $40,000 and $60,000 for an assistant coach at a four-year program. Head strength and conditioning coaches at the higher four-year institutions are typically paid anywhere from $45,000 to $75,000 annually. Strength and conditioning coaches at the professional levels typically earn more than college coaches, but usually less than $100,000 per year.

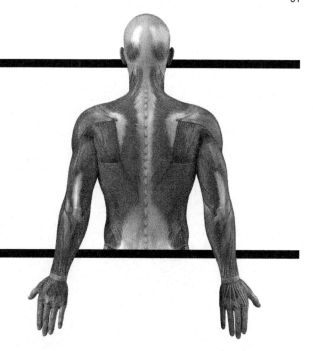

CHAPTER 7
Teaching Careers

What is a teacher and what role does this profession play with regards to the field of kinesiology? A teacher is a professionally trained educator who provides the ability to help others learn a specific topic of interest. The employment title of "teacher" is extremely vague, similarly to the profession of "coaching" since everyone does some aspect or confirms to a style of leadership towards directing a team or a set of individuals. Perhaps, it won't be exactly the same premise but for the sake of seeking and obtaining a good career, let's focus on the true nature of what the profession of a "teacher" is, the level and age groups involved, and what the requirements are to have a successful teaching career that kinesiology majors can consider.

Elementary Teaching Careers in the Field of Kinesiology

Teaching motor skills to children was the main focus for regimented K-6 grade school programs after World War II. The ability to have coordination and proper mechanics of movement was the focus behind the discipline of physical education, which has now developed into one of the subdisciplines in kinesiology. Over the years, this assignment has been given to elementary education teachers who don't have the background to perform this duty, based on the lack of finances of the school district. Other school districts will hire a part-time PE specialist who will perform the instruction on a part-time basis. Budget cuts have hurt certain traditional programs that result in poor curriculum being taught in some school districts today. The goal would be to find school districts that have a full-time physical educator who teaches curriculum that will assist with motor skills such as hopping, skipping, and throwing before sports are introduced. Figures 7.1 and 7.2 displays the states that have hired elementary school teachers and salary scales as of May 2013.

Figure 7.1:

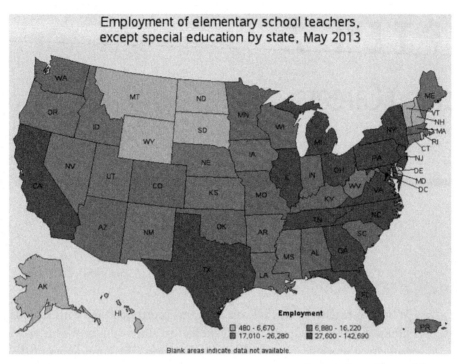

Source: http://www.bls.gov

Figure 7.2:

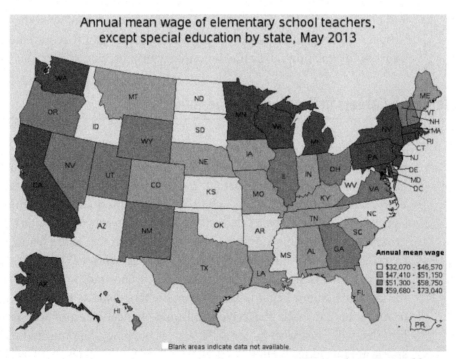

Source: http://www.bls.gov

Secondary Teaching Careers in the Field of Kinesiology

Secondary physical educators are employed at the middle and high school levels in education. Their main purpose is not focusing on primary or basic motor skills like primary or elementary physical educators but on sport-based activities and fitness-related improvements with pre-pubescent to pubescent age groups. The focus should be on improving the concept of teamwork and cooperation, developing leadership, and accomplishing individual and team goals through fitness or movement-related curriculum.

Important Qualities of Primary and Secondary Physical Educators

1. **Communication skills.** Physical educators provide instruction and organization, and motivate their students so they must develop excellent communication skills. Effective communication will ensure proper techniques, strategies, and rules of either the sport or motor skill so all participants will fully comprehend the information provided.
2. **Decision-making skills.** Physical educators must select the strategy to use toward teaching the skill or providing cues that will help improve learning at the next level of progression.
3. **Dedication.** Physical educators must be available before, during, and after to facilitate the individual students in improving physical and motor skills.
4. **Interpersonal skills.** Physical educators should be able to relate well to others in order to foster positive relationships and help develop the concept of teamwork through this important characteristic.
5. **Leadership skills.** Physical educators must have good leadership skills to motivate and push students to overcome obstacles. They must be leaders at all facets of instruction.
6. **Resourcefulness.** Physical educators must take all available facets of the skills listed above to achieve the best chances of having their students succeed in developing their motor skills and have an appreciation of movement as a wellness component.
7. **Patience.** Elementary-level physical educators need to have the ability to tolerate uncooperative or unskilled students based on their upbringing or lack of experiences. Underachieving students need guidance to feel comfortable around their peers and a patient physical educator can create this environment for all children to experience enjoyment through movement activities.

Job Duties of a Primary and Secondary Physical Education Teacher

- Plan appropriate progressive lessons that teach students motor skills, teamwork, and strategy.
- Assess students to evaluate their current motor skills and fitness levels.
- Teach productive lessons in the amount of time given with regards to large or small class sizes.
- Grade students' motor skills to monitor their progress and prepare to report these outcomes to parents and the school administrator.
- Communicate with parents about their child's progress and if proactive steps are necessary and what these steps would be.
- Work with students individually to help them with motor or skill-related movements.
- Prepare students for promoting physical activity as a daily routine within their family life structure.
- Develop and enforce discipline to teach children about following and abiding by rules through games and sport activities.
- Supervise students during pre-start times, lunchtime, or other activities that would require an adult presence for safety, health, and overall welfare of all school participants.

Work Environment for Primary and Secondary Physical Educators

Primary and secondary physical educators are employed in public and private sectors all across the country. Having an opportunity to create changes and assist students with improving their education is very rewarding. However, this profession can be very stressful for many reasons such as work conditions, student discipline issues, or financial concerns of the school district. Some school districts will have large class sizes and outdated technology, such as computers and software programs. Many teachers are held accountable for students' standardized test scores, which lead to additional stress on the job. Some primary and secondary teachers operate on a traditional 10-month contract, allowing a 2-month summer break. Others will be employed in school districts with a year-round schedule typically 8 weeks straight then 1 week off, before starting a cycle, including 5-week midwinter break. This is based on either overcrowding issues or lack of facilities based on the school district's budget and operational policies.

The work schedules for primary and secondary physical educators are generally during regular school hours. There will be opportunities that some hours may be earlier or later based on meetings with parents, students, and other teachers. Evenings and weekends are spent on grading papers and preparing lessons. Extra assignments could be given during the summer months or after school for extracurricular activities such as supervising student clubs or sport teams that would be compensated separately.

Employment Outlook for Primary and Secondary Physical Educators

According to the Board of Labor Statistics May 2013 Report, primary and secondary educators held about 1.5 million jobs in 2013 (Figure 7.3). High school teachers held about 955,800 jobs in 2013 but it is unknown how many physical and health educators were employed that year nationally. The median annual wage for primary level educators was $50,120 in May 2013. The median wage is the wage at which half the workers in an occupation earned more than that amount and half earned less. The lowest 10% earned less than $32,450, and the top 10% earned more than $78,230. The median annual wage for secondary school educators was $53,400. The lowest 10% earned less than $35,630, and the top 10% earned more than $83,160 (Figure 7.4). Most states have tenure laws if they belong to a teacher union which affiliates themselves with the National Teachers Association (NEA). Tenure is associated with job security for life once you have passed a probationary period of two to three years of satisfactory evaluations from your principal or supervisors. Currently, this concept is being challenged by school administrators based on the inability to remove tenured teachers who are not continuing satisfactory levels of performance on an annual basis.

Training, CEUs, Degree, License, Advancement Education Requirements for Primary or Secondary Teachers

Primary and secondary physical educators will need a bachelor's degree in physical education or some kinesiology-related field since all states require public high school teachers to have this degree. Most states require high school teachers to have majored in an accredited NCATE (National Council for Accreditation of Teacher Education) preparatory curriculum. While majoring in either physical education or kinesiology, future teachers typically enroll in an accredited teacher preparation program and take additional coursework in education theory and child psychology as well. In teacher education programs, prospective high school teachers learn how to present information to students and how to work with students of varying abilities and backgrounds. Programs typically include fieldwork, such as student teaching. For information about teacher preparation programs in your state, visit http://www.Teach.org.

All states require teachers in public schools to be licensed or certified. Those who teach in private schools are generally not required to be licensed. Some states require high school teachers to earn a master's degree or progress towards more educational training coursework after earning their teaching certification.

High school physical educators typically are awarded a secondary teaching credential or high school certification. This allows them the ability to teach from middle school to the senior high school levels. These requirements will always differ from state to state. Depending on which state you intend to work in, completing a semester to year-long supervised teaching experience under a licensed teacher supervisor is mandated. Some states require a certain GPA to gain teacher candidacy into the teacher education program, usually during your junior year in college. Many states will also require student teacher candidates to take and pass an exam that demonstrates general academic prowess and their knowledge in physical education/kinesiology. For information on certification requirements in your state, visit http://www.Teach.org.

Often, primary and secondary physical educators are required to complete annual professional development classes to maintain their teaching licensure. Most states require teachers to pass a criminal background check, and some states require teachers to complete a master's degree after receiving their certification. All states offer an alternative route to certification for people who already have a bachelor's degree but lack the education courses required for certification. Some alternative certification programs allow candidates to begin teaching immediately under the supervision of an experienced teacher. These programs cover teaching methods and child development. After they complete the program, student teacher candidates are awarded their teacher certification in the subject matter and level.

Two- or Four-Year Institutions of Higher Education

As stated in Chapter 6, there are thousands of public and private colleges or universities all across this country. According to the U.S. Department of Education Report (2013), there are 7,021 colleges and universities in the United States. Of these, 1,729 two-year degree institutions existed and 2,870 four-year degree schools were accounted for. All provide offerings of employment on a regular basis if you have the background and experience. There were 17,487,475 students enrolled in degree-seeking programs back in 2005. Two-year community or junior colleges have different requirements than four-year institutions. As stated in Chapter 1, there are over 870 kinesiology or related programs currently in the United States. It is common for kinesiology-prepared students to teach beyond K-12 and pursue employment at the community college or a four-year institution as long as they meet hiring requirements of that institution. Postsecondary instructors work at different types of institutions so their job duties will vary, based on what type of higher education level they work for. Some postsecondary instructors are called professors who work for large state universities. At this level, the expectation for these faculty members is to perform research or experiments and applying for grants to fund these projects. The focus is less on teaching compared to smaller colleges or lower levels such as two-year institutions. Some instructors use web-based curriculum to teach and present their lesson plans. They communicate with students by email or through discussion folders and do not physically meet with their students in person. Let's take a look at needed characteristics to possess if you decide to pursue a career as a community college or university professor.

Figure 7.3:

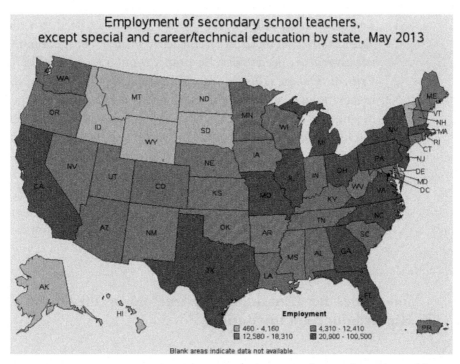

Source: http://www.bls.gov

Figure 7.4:

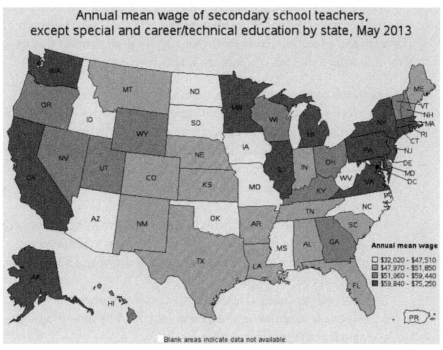

Source: http://www.bls.gov

Qualities of a Community College or University Professor

1. *Communication skills.* Postsecondary instructors need to write papers, provide lectures, and serve on several department or college committees. To do so effectively, they need to develop proper communication skills.
2. *Critical-thinking skills.* In order to challenge students in class and with assignments through conducting research and designing proper experiments, postsecondary instructors need to develop good critical-thinking skills.
3. *Resourcefulness.* Postsecondary instructors need to be flexible and use different learning techniques that will facilitate learning. All students will have different learning styles so keeping options open and available is recommended.
4. *Writing skills.* Most four-year college professors need to publish original research and present their findings to their peers through professional conferences. This quality is a necessity for those who want to pursue careers at research institutions or similar.

Job Duties for Kinesiology Instructors or Professors at Two-Year Higher Education Institutions

Your teaching assignment is based on your educational experience or specialty area you possess. Most two-year schools would require a kinesiology-based master's degree. A full teaching load, depending upon the faculty contract and union agreements, would consist of teaching 15 to 18 hours of physical activity courses and sport theory classes per week. Personal health or wellness lecture classes are common nationwide as a general education requirement for all college students at this level. As for duties, the following duties are common among two-year institutions:

1. Teach courses in the subject area of interest or need.
2. Work with students who are either studying for a degree, taking certificate or certification classes in this area, or are there to improve their general knowledge.
3. Develop new instructional curriculum for the department to promote student needs or improve enrollment.
4. Update lesson plans and assignments to maintain standards and curriculum currency.
5. Work with your department colleagues to develop or modify the curriculum to fit the needs of the students who are majoring in kinesiology.
6. Assess students' progress by providing accurate and adequate grading methods for each course taught.
7. Advise these students about which classes to enroll in as well as career planning.
8. Maintain currency in the kinesiology field by attending seminars or professional development activities.
9. Serve on academic and administrative committees.

Job Duties for Kinesiology Instructors or Professors at Four-Year Higher Education Institutions

At four-year colleges and universities, professors may teach a minimum of two and a maximum of five courses per semester, depending upon the annual teaching contract negotiated with the faculty union. Professors may have large class sizes, depending upon the type of course and the population of the institution. Smaller or private four-year schools have low student ratios to instructor. Professors should maintain current changes in their field by following research articles in their field and by attending professional conferences. To gain tenure, usually a six-year process of demonstrating competence in research, teaching, and service that ensures job security and productivity is a must during this time period. Two-year schools will sometimes have a tenure process after two or three years; however, the requirements are not as stringent or critical compared to their four-year counterparts. As for duties, the following duties are common among four-year institutions:

1. Teach courses in the subject area of interest or need.
2. Work with students who are either studying for a bachelor's degree, taking graduate coursework, or are there to improve their general knowledge.
3. Develop new instructional curriculum for the department to promote student needs or improve enrollment.
4. Update lesson plans and assignments to maintain standards and curriculum currency.
5. Work with your department colleagues to develop or modify the curriculum to fit the needs of the students who are majoring in kinesiology.
6. Assess students' progress by providing accurate and adequate grading methods for each course taught.
7. Advise these students about which classes to enroll in as well as career planning.
8. Maintain currency in the kinesiology field by attending seminars or professional development activities.
9. Serve on academic and administrative committees.
10. Conduct research, present findings at appropriate venues, and apply for grants to support these lines.
11. Supervise undergraduate and graduate students who are pursuing kinesiology-related degrees.
12. Publish your research in peer-reviewed academic journals in the kinesiology field.

Postsecondary Work Environment

According to the Board of Labor and Statistics, 1,267,000 people were employed in postsecondary teaching, 75% of postsecondary instructors worked at four-year colleges, universities, and professional schools in 2012; 21% worked at community or junior colleges. The remaining 4% worked for technical or private trade schools, business schools, or management training facilities. Working hours are not the typical 9 to 5 as other jobs and are flexible, based on your level of seniority among your colleagues and specialty. The majority of the time is spent in the classroom or providing student contact availability at a central location within the department, called office hours. The remaining amount of time is spent performing research, grading exams or papers, and providing service through committee assignments as a representative to the department, school, or college.

Professors must be able to find a balance between teaching their courses, performing scholarly works through research, and providing representation through service efforts. This can be a challenge, especially for junior faculty members seeking promotion and tenure at four-year universities. At the two-year institutions, the balance is between teaching classes and providing service to the department. The majority of classes are offered during the day, some are offered during the evening hours or online to accommodate students who work full time or have other obligations. A majority of faculty do not teach during the summer months for extra pay, spending their time on other projects or research writing. The time off is considered a perk to those who want this type of flexibility in their life.

Job Outlook for Two- and Four-Year College Professors

Postsecondary teachers held 1,267,000 jobs in 2012. The median annual wage for postsecondary instructors was $68,970, based on the Bureau of Labor Statistics Report dated May 2012. The median wage is the wage at which half the workers in an occupation earned more than that amount and half earned less. The lowest 10% earned less than $35,670, and the top 10% earned more than $142,270. Wages can vary by institution type and by state (Figure 7.5). Postsecondary instructors have the ability to obtain higher wages in colleges, universities, and professional schools compared to community colleges or other types of schools. There are exceptions where this is not the case in certain states that have strong faculty unions at the two-year system.

Employment opportunities for postsecondary instructors are expected to increase 19% from 2012 to 2022, both part-time and full-time postsecondary instructors are included with this prediction (Figures 7.6 and 7.7). This increase is based on growth expectations due to enrollment figures at postsecondary institutions. As numbers improve for incoming students in the next 10 years, more postsecondary instructors will be hired to create availability for individual institutions that compete for these students. Also, depending upon the status of the economy and the political nature of our government, this plays an important role towards providing additional funds given to hire more faculty members at two- and four-year schools. In all categories of education including kinesiology, many of the new positions will be offered at part-time employment or non-tenure-track since healthcare and benefit programs become an extra cost among higher education employers. Retirements will create additional openings for new professors. It would be speculative at this time to assume these openings will be offered at a tenure-track position or become part time or term contracts, meaning year-to-year renewals.

Two- and Four-Year Postsecondary Teacher Training, CEUs, Educational Requirements

Educational requirements for postsecondary teaching in kinesiology are pretty consistent with most institutions nationwide. A master's degree in the discipline is a minimum requirement at most community colleges or technical schools even though some will make an exception with a bachelor's degree in kinesiology and a certification or other related experience that would provide an equivalency to a master's degree. Postsecondary instructors who want to work for four-year public state institutions are required to have an earned doctoral degree in their discipline. However, some universities could hire those candidates who have a master's degree with the understanding that they will complete a doctoral degree within a certain time limit in order to qualify for a tenure-track position. Doctoral degree programs are not offered at all institutions of higher education and generally take four to seven years to complete. The *Chronicles of Higher Education* reported several years back that 60% of students who are accepted into a doctoral program do not finish or complete their studies. Besides taking research-based coursework in the field, writing a doctoral dissertation based on the area of selected original research is required before the degree is granted.

Some colleges or universities may prefer to hire faculty who have prior successful teaching history but this is not always the case for all institutions. Some prospective candidates can gain teaching experience by working as a teaching assistant. This is a title given to graduate students who are enrolled in an accredited graduate program and teach courses to supplement the scholarship or money they have been awarded by the institution. Others may ask for sample publications to ensure that the candidate does have a strong background with completing research projects and successfully writing the manuscript well enough to be accepted into an academic peer-reviewed journal.

Figure 7.5:

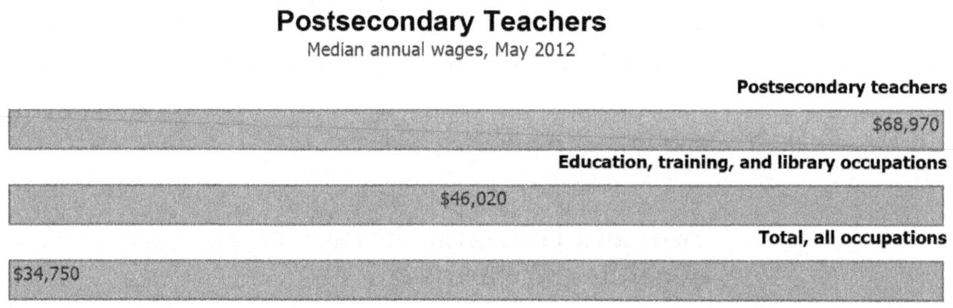

Postsecondary Teachers

Median annual wages, May 2012

Postsecondary teachers

$68,970

Education, training, and library occupations

$46,020

Total, all occupations

$34,750

Note: All Occupations includes all occupations in the U.S. Economy.

Source: U.S. Bureau of Labor Statistics, Occupational Employment Statistics, 2013

For entry-level college professors, a major goal to achieve after being hired is to obtain tenure. This term was discussed earlier in this chapter guaranteeing that you cannot be fired from your postsecondary position without just cause. Tenure for most institutions takes about seven years to accomplish, meaning you are submitting your portfolio during your sixth year of service to that institution. Tenure is granted through a review of the candidate's research, contribution to the institution, and teaching. However, many institutions are depending on limited-term or part-time faculty contracts due to fiscal issues, so teaching positions on a "tenure track" are declining. Tenure is not always associated with one's academic rank. Sometimes, an instructor applies for rank and tenure at the same time but not always. The academic ranking system usually starts with the level of an assistant professor. The next rank would be an associate professor, leading to the highest rank of a full professor. Many professors will work at an institution for decades and not achieve the last rank. Each level requires a standard of performance that must be accomplished and judged among your fellow peers at the college or university. This committee, usually the Promotion and Tenure Committee, will decide if your body of work qualifies you for this academic title and salary increase.

Some tenured professors decide to advance into an administrative position such as a department chair, associate dean, or even higher. Of course, these positions require a length of service as a tenured faculty member and usually a rank of an associate professor or higher. The upside towards transitioning to this position is a higher salary and a reduced or no teaching load. The downside to this type of administrative post require more time commitment (11-month contract or longer), less flexibility with your schedule, and the inability to spend time with students in the classroom or research opportunities.

Figure 7.6:

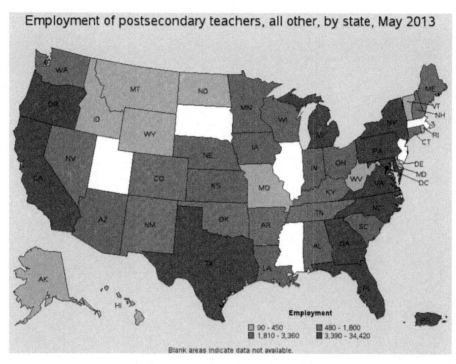

Source: http://www.bls.gov

Figure 7.7:

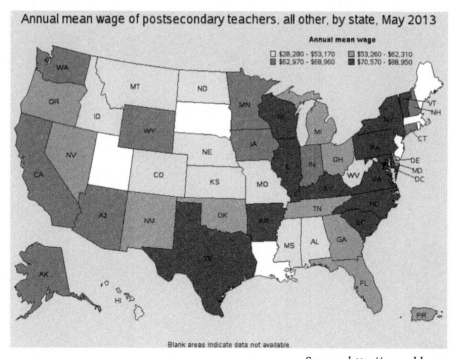

Source: http://www.bls.gov

CHAPTER 8

Sport Management Careers

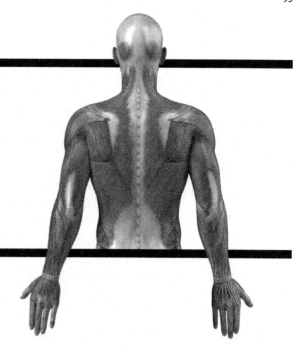

The area of this discipline is relatively new if you look historically at the origin of this major or specialization. Historically, the principles of management have always been considered a "business" concept and taught under this organizational umbrella. However, since professional sports have become a $451 billion industry, employment specialties have emerged just as other kinesiology career paths that have been discussed in past chapters have. The evolution of physical activity in a business sense is another inclusion to the field of kinesiology. Sport management, the concept, and the career choices this field offers will be discussed throughout this chapter.

What Is Sport Management?

The sports industry in the United States has been evolving since the start of professional sports in the mid to late 1800s. How a professional team organizes itself through the concept of management practices has also changed drastically. The exposure of radio, television, and now the Internet has created a feeding frenzy of millions of viewers or fans who follow organized sports venues that is no longer focused on professional leagues or specific sports. Revenue obtained from professional sports beyond ticket sales from the past 50 years has quickly developed this industry into a worldwide phenomenon with a revenue stream of over $400 billion. What used to justify the ability to watch sporting events, based on increased leisure time, is no longer the answer. The proliferation of cell phone or tablet access to streaming media or box scores has contributed to additional millions of people having access to information that can drive additional revenue from the consumer to the business venue. Also, with increased information access, this also drives the consumer to reach out to physical venues such as golf courses, tennis clubs, amateur and minor leagues, and professional sporting events and purchase services that will allow jobs in this area to be offered and filled. Such jobs or professions now include the following in the area of sport management:

1. Facility Management
2. Sport Marketing
3. Sales and Promotions
4. Sport Information Directors
5. Athletic or Recreational Directors
6. Sport Equipment Sales
7. Public Relations for Local, Regional, National, or International Venues
8. Sport Sponsorships
9. Sport Agents
10. Event Management
11. Compliance within Sport Leagues (Professional or Amateur)

Currently, there are over 200 sport management undergraduate programs or specializations being offered at colleges and universities in the United States. As mentioned in Chapter 1, finding a good sport management program should focus on the following key areas:

1. Applicable coursework in the area of sport management
2. Gaining relevant experience within the coursework and faculty members
3. Finding an internship that will provide additional experience that cannot be obtained through the coursework
4. Obtaining practical experience throughout your four-year coursework in sport management
5. Seeking volunteer experience through peer, faculty, or sage mentorships that can improve your chances for obtaining a better internship experience and/or job opportunities

During this chapter discussion, the focus will be on certain sport management professions that are more popular than others. By no means is this stating you should be pursuing only the areas that are highlighted. Use the faculty and networking resources to obtain additional information if you choose to seek other areas of employment in this field of study in kinesiology. Information constantly changes within several months as does your interest based on experiences or observations. Of all the listed sport management professions listed earlier, the top three are (1) Facility and Event Management, (2) Intercollegiate Athletics, and (3) Professional Sports. Let's start with one of the most popular sport management professions, called Facility and Event Management.

Facility and Event Management in Sport Management

There are thousands of facilities and events offered across this country that hire qualified personnel to manage or oversee a certain recreational, athletic, or public event facility, such as city or county camp grounds, park and recreation sites, aquatic centers, or other public or private sport venues. From entry-level management to the CEO (chief operations officer) of a major sports venue, students need to know what is available and what types of facilities could be potential career opportunities. Starting with local park and recreation sites are common among college hires. These positions exist in every city or town all across the country. Recreation management personnel held about 345,400 positions nationwide, according to the Board of Labor Statistics Report from 2012. Park and recreation departments consisted of 43% of the facility management positions; 16% were hired at hospital-based or rehabilitation facilities; 12% from professional sport or similar organizations; 10% were employed in the arts and entertainment industry that focused on recreational themes; and the rest were in other public or private sectors that were non-profits or profit-based athletic camps or facilities.

Qualities of a Sport or Event Facility Manager

According to the Bureau of Labor Statistics, U.S. Department of Labor, Occupational Outlook Handbook, 2014-15 Edition, all facility managers at athletic or sport-related venues are recommended to possess the following characteristics in order for them to be highly successful in this career field.

Communication skills. Sport or event management facility personnel must be able to communicate effectively. They speak to large audiences, may they be employees or attendees. Clear instructions in order to maintain health and safety are needed at the facility at all times.

Flexibility. Planning activities and the nature of changing environments within the facility will occur. They will need to adapt accordingly to weather, crowds, equipment, and other changes that create challenges when supervising a facility and large groups of people.

Leadership skills. When in charge of a facility of sport venue, you will have to promote skilled managerial techniques to both large and small groups. Effective leadership and managing of all sorts of personalities, disabilities, and learning skills will be called upon at any facility or sport site.

Physical strength. Sport or event management facility personnel should be physically fit. There will be times where besides managing staff, you will be called upon to assist with physical tasks such as moving equipment and relocating items that will require considerable lifting.

Problem-solving skills. Leaders in this field need to possess strong problem-solving skills. Besides demonstrating flexibility with the environment, making tough and rational decisions will be called upon to prevent further issues in the near future. Tough decisions that develop into success stories usually do not solve the problems right away. Through quick and practical thinking, taking the blame early on but knowing it will lead to success in the future becomes an ethical decision that not all leaders are willing to make.

Job Duties of a Sport or Event Facility Manager

Sport or event facility managers typically do the following:

1. Supervise staff with regards to organizing daily planned events at the facility.
2. Train staff for performing a variety of roles in order to ensure a smooth transition for every event.
3. Enforce rules and regulations to promote health and safety for staff and attendees/participants.
4. Modify venues to ensure compliance for special needs.
5. Enforce federal laws and guidelines for facilities and treatment of participants, etc.
6. Order and inventory equipment as well as create regular inspections of equipment and facilities to reduce liability and negligence to the organization or facility site.
7. Teach or promote continuing education for staff and other workers to maintain safety and health standards within the facility.
8. Screen and hire appropriate and qualified employees.

The responsibilities will vary greatly with regards to facility site, level of authority, past experience, training protocol in place, and the local or state mandates or laws. Other responsibilities could be administering activities directly, fundraising, public relations campaigning, and community service contributions.

Work Environment

Facility or event management workers are employed in a variety of settings, including indoor or outdoor sport venues, convention halls or centers, outdoor camps, recreation centers, hotel spas and resorts, and even on cruise ships. They may also work in hospital or rehabilitation centers. Event directors and facility supervisors typically spend most of their time indoors in an office setting, planning or supervising programs or special events.

Employment Outlook

Future employment forecasting is demonstrating available positions since event management doesn't necessarily mean sport or athletic events. This could be car shows, concerts, trade shows, etc. As the economy recovers, more people will have extra income to spend on discretionary entertainment that has a personal appeal to them. The median annual wages for facility or event management workers based on the May 2012 Bureau of Labor Statistics shows an annual salary at $34,750. Recreational management workers tend to make less money but the benefits of working for a town, city, or government entity can make up for a lower wage than a private venue. Arts, entertainment, and recreation start at a lower salary $19,320, and these types of positions might not be set hours, working weekends, irregular hours, or seasonally employed. The percent change in future employment projected over the next decade is (2012-22) is showing an 11% increase over previous years' predictions.

Employment of recreation workers is projected to grow 14% from 2012 to 2022, about as fast as the average for all occupations (Figures 8.1 and 8.2). In response to growing rates of childhood obesity, a number of federal, state, and local campaigns have been established to encourage young people to be physically active. As more emphasis is placed on the importance of exercise, more recreation workers will be needed to work in fitness centers, sports centers, and camps specializing in younger participants.

Event and Facility Management Training, CEUs, Educational Requirements

Event and facility management employees require at least a four-year degree. Although there are employees who have an educational background from an associate's degree to doctoral degrees, the type of degree is preferred for these kind of positions. It is not always a necessity to have bachelor's degree in kinesiology-related programs such as recreation or leisure studies. Specific coursework focusing on management methods, human development, community organization, supervision of employees, and business administration are required. Students should take courses in developing programs for all types of populations (children, older adults, disabilities, etc.). Students may choose to specialize in specific areas of recreation management, outdoor recreation, industrial wellness, and outdoor management. A bachelor's degree in public administration or a minor in business may help applicants qualify for event and facility management. Obtaining a master's degree will separate you from other candidates along with obtaining a supervisory certification with different combinations of education and work experience. Some recreational site positions will require a national certification for national and state parks.

As event and facility managers gain additional experience, they may be promoted to positions with higher responsibilities. Recreational managers with work experience and managerial skills may advance to higher positions. Eventually, they may become a director for a city or park setting or may branch off and work for corporations that specialize in outdoor recreation products.

Future Outlook for Sport Management Event and Facility Personnel

With regards to many recreational positions available, job prospects will be best for those seeking part-time, seasonal, or temporary openings. Because these jobs tend to be transitional and held by part-timers, this could allow for more full-time positions when transitional workers do leave the jobsite, thus creating more job openings. Workers with bachelor's or master's degrees related to kinesiology should have better chances at securing these positions. Volunteer experience, having a background performing administrative tasks, including facility management and record-keeping and information management, will remain extremely valuable against those who lack these specific skills. Event and facility managers will be needed to facilitate or assist with new growth or developments among the organization or team.

In addition, event and facility staff will be in greater demand if they have a focus on the environmental impact and energy efficiency of the buildings they manage. Understanding how to improve energy efficiency does reduce costs and often is required by state or federal regulations. Having a further understanding of building codes and what is considered compliant within your regions is a plus. Teams and organizations also are expected to have more event or facility staff, as opposed to using people who manage several facilities on a contract basis but have no expertise. This will create demand for a larger total number of event and facility managers, leading to stronger growth for this field in sport management.

Intercollegiate Sport Management

Collegiate sport is another attractive area of sport management for career paths. In the past as stated earlier in this chapter, many of these positions were business-minded or trained employees who didn't have a background in sport or kinesiology. The trend has now changed over the past several decades where many of these positions find the connection between business and sport more advantageous due to the passion and enthusiasm that allows career-minded people to connect with their goals, leading to a successful and enjoyable profession.

There are many jobs and positions available for sport management students in the realm of intercollegiate sport. I will cover these main career opportunities and want you to understand that once you start exploring this area of interest further, you might find other areas of interest not listed in this chapter but available as a career, leading to a successful profession.

1. Administrative Positions
2. Marketing/Promotions
3. Facility Operations
4. Equipment Management

Administrative Positions in Intercollegiate Sport Management

These types of positions include the senior management staff for the athletic department for either the college or university and can include the senior athletic director, lower-level athletic directors, and assistants to the athletic director, including graduate assistants, secretarial staff, and compliance officers. Their ability to become quickly employed may be based on the following skill sets:

1. Analytical—Synthesizes complex information; uses intuition and experience to complement data
2. Problem Solving—Identifies and resolves problems in a timely manner; gathers and analyzes information skillfully; develops alternative solutions; works well in group problem solving situations; uses reason even when dealing with emotional topics

Figure 8.1:

Source: http://www.bls.gov

3. Technical Skills—Top-notch computer literacy; strives to continuously build knowledge and skills
4. Oral Communication—Speaks clearly and persuasively in positive or negative situations; ability to follow oral and written instructions
5. Written Communication—Writes clearly and concisely; grammar perfectionist
6. Ethics—Treats people with respect; keeps commitments; works with integrity and honesty; upholds organizational values
7. Innovation—Displays original thinking and creativity; meets challenges with resourcefulness
8. Professionalism—Reacts well under pressure; follows through on commitments and makes sound and thoughtful business decisions

Essential Job Duties and Responsibilities for Intercollegiate Administrative Sport Management

- Oversee heavy calendaring for daily operations and meetings
- Manage complex domestic and possible international travel and logistics
- Screen heavy incoming and outgoing phone calls, responding appropriately
- Manage expense reports and corporate spending deductions
- Coordinate with internal and external executives and assistants to coordinate events, meetings, and appointments
- Prepare meeting materials, booklets, and other documents associated with the administration of sport supervision and championships. Assist with coordination of travel for representatives of member institutions to attend championships and meetings
- Provide administrative support to officiating coordinators as assigned by the manager and assist with management of online officiating programs including detailed data entry, schedule review and maintenance, payment database entry and review, facilitation of contract mailing, and collection. Assist with keeping databases current and monitoring changes to data, calendar, or playing schedules
- Assist with specific liaison television assignments as assigned
- Provide a sense of urgency when solving problems and making sound independent decisions under pressure
- Ability to work overtime as needed, evenings or weekends during times of high workload or emergency situations
- Other duties as assigned

Qualifications for Intercollegiate Administrative Sport Management Positions/Training, CEUs, Educational Requirements

If you are wondering about the minimum requirements to become the senior athletic director for a college or university, here are the qualifications needed: First, you must have four to five years of experience working as an administrative assistant, under senior management or similar administrative role at a four-year school. Having a working knowledge of administrative and clerical procedures and systems is important. Excellent written communication and interpersonal skills allow you to be a leader and have the ability to supervise staff fairly. You must have knowledge of intercollegiate sports and a working knowledge of particular computer software that connects you with the division or athletic league officials. A master's degree in the field of kinesiology, sport management, or business-related field is the minimum educational requirements even though some four-year school administrators hold doctorate degrees in administrative or higher education and/or leadership. Other lower division intercollegiate administrative positions would require a minimum of a bachelor's degree with the ability to have a working knowledge of what is needed to gain further experience in order to move up in this competitive market by observing the skills and traits required to eventually reach the top management position in intercollegiate athletics at a college or university.

Marketing and Promotion Positions in Intercollegiate Athletics

These types of positions include the sales staff for the athletic department for either the college or university and can include planning strategies on how to effectively improve the exposure and improve income for the university through the athletic programs. Promotion managers develop advertising pricing with companies or corporate sponsorships, expand the branding of the teams, and other incentive programs. Associate level staffers report directly to their managers who are in charge of publicizing the athletic brand of the institution. Field representatives are considered the entry-level marketing and promotion positions that require minimal training. Figures 8.3 and 8.4 shows which states employ marketing managers nationally and their salary scale. Their ability to become quickly employed may be based on the following skill sets:

1. Understanding database marketing and analytics
2. Possessing a passion for creating, implementing, and energizing a professional sales force
3. A proven entrepreneur who enjoys challenge and is skilled in marketing, sales, and communications techniques
4. Demonstrative athletics-fan relationship
5. Experience to oversee the day-to-day initiatives related to ticket sales, marketing, and sales strategies

Essential Job Duties and Responsibilities for Intercollegiate Marketing and Promotions

- Database marketing
- Create and advance the integration of customer-service relationship

Figure 8.2:

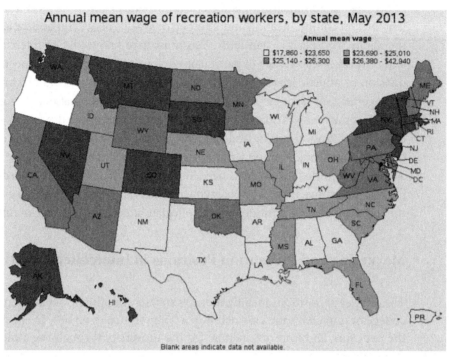

Source: http://www.bls.gov

Figure 8.3:

Source: http://www.bls.gov

Figure 8.4:

Source: http://www.bls.gov

- Develop, implement, and evaluate initiative to transition database users into season ticket sales
- Streamline the online customer purchase experience
- Develop reports to assist director in evaluating sales performance (team and individual basis)

Intercollegiate Athletics Sport Marketing and Promotion Training, CEUs, Educational Requirements

A minimum of a bachelor's degree in kinesiology with a specialization in sport management, communications, business, or statistics is required for these types of positions. A graduate degree in business with emphasis in marketing or sales is preferred. A minimum of two years working in the field of sport marketing is essential for many intercollegiate athletic departments. Additional experience or knowledge of database and digital marketing strategies would be highly desirable in these professions. Having organization and time management skills from prior internships or previous positions would be helpful. Even in these positions, demonstrating a team leadership role allows the employers to seek these types of individuals for their programs.

Facility Operations in Intercollegiate Athletics

The department of intercollegiate athletics at several institutions in the United States consists of more than 250 staff members and coaches and provides 25 or more varsity sports programs. These programs could include more than 850 student-athletes who participate in various sports within the National Collegiate Athletic Association (NCAA) annually. With the amount of student-athletes, and the type of sport, use of facilities would be a huge undertaking. Consider the winter, spring, and fall seasons, including unofficial and official practices times, game day preparation, and weekend work. The amount of organization and responsibilities for coordinating these events would be challenging for anyone.

Essential Job Duties and Responsibilities for Facility Operations in Intercollegiate Athletics

This position performs maintenance and related functions to athletic fields/venues in support of athletic department programs and activities. Scope includes traditional maintenance and repairs to athletic facilities and equipment as well as preventive maintenance at athletic department fields and sports venues. These positions provide significant support for student-athletes, coaches, and spectators through a variety of general tasks related to home events, athletic equipment, and fan amenities. Following are potential daily job duties and responsibilities for facilities operations personnel:

- Perform special event and program support tasks including setup and takedown of practice and game equipment such as baskets, nets, goals, timing systems, banners, tables, chairs, public address systems, etc. Participate in activity transitions (all athletic sports) as well as event setups in meeting rooms.
- Supervise preparation of field surfaces such as painting field lines and preparing adjacent areas for field events, if needed.
- Assist with the takedown or cleanup of event venues.

Facility Operations Intercollegiate Athletics Training, CEUs, Educational Requirements

With regards to meeting the qualifications for facilities operations for a four-year intercollegiate athletic program, any combination of education, technical training, and work experience is required. A basic understanding is required of maintenance practices, methods, procedures, equipment, tools, materials, and proper sequencing of the required steps in structuring and completing grounds-keeping work and assigned projects. Candidates should have be ability to operate machines and equipment used for maintenance and repair of athletic flooring, especially artificial turf. Ability to communicate clearly and effectively in person and having knowledge of safe work practices would be an expectation based on experience and past training at another athletic facility. To qualify for a supervisor or manager role, a bachelor's degree in a related field of study, past history of being a team leader in some facility operation capacity, having an understanding of grounds-keeping experience including methods, processes, materials used in performing building maintenance work external relations, sales, etc. are all considered assets towards obtaining this next level career step.

Equipment Management in Intercollegiate Athletics

An assistant or equipment manager is responsible for equipment safety standards, policy, compliance, and inventory. The equipment manager would be under the general supervision of an athletic director and assist with the overall equipment operation of the varsity sports to include the involvement with both men's and women's programs. This position would also be responsible for supervising assistants and student workers. Depending upon the four-year school, an athletic department could have over 30 varsity sport programs, including more than 800-plus student-athletes who participate in various programs throughout the academic calendar. Besides ordering equipment for the athletic department on behalf of the particular sport, there are other major responsibilities that are placed upon this important position.

Essential Job Duties and Responsibilities for Equipment Management in Intercollegiate Athletics

As stated earlier, this position requires an extremely organized and efficient person. When you are working with many athletic teams and individuals, truly understand the importance of this position and what is really needed to succeed in this career path. Possessing problem-solving skills, allowing one to multitask, work with frequent interruptions, and be an effective listener are highly coveted. Highly effective verbal and written communication skills in the English language are expected. The ideal candidate must be proficient in the use of basic computer applications. Customer service–focused attitude and ability to work with a diverse work group is important. This candidate must be organized and have the ability to work in a fast-paced environment with rapidly changing deadlines and multiple priorities. Here are some of the listed responsibilities:

- Maintain inventory records for all assigned athletic sport teams.
- Fit student-athletes with proper size of equipment and uniforms and check for damage.
- Work closely with assigned coaches, advising them regarding the purchase, issue, and return of assigned athletic equipment.
- Supervise and account for the issue, return, storage, and maintenance of the equipment assigned to the intercollegiate student-athletes.
- Coordinate laundry to implement process for all practice, game clothing, and uniforms for team practices and games for each assigned sport.

- Work directly with representatives from outside vendors to research, select, and purchase clothing and equipment for sport teams that fit the university's philosophy and mission.
- Respond to inquiries and requests from members of senior staff and donors to the athletic programs that involve equipment or athletic gear.

Equipment Management Intercollegiate Athletics Training, CEUs, Educational Requirements

A bachelor's degree in kinesiology or equivalent is required for this position. Prior experience working in equipment management at an intercollegiate athletic organization is expected. Having a successful internship experience or similar, at a lower-level division or smaller schools could be substituted for the former. The candidate must have thorough knowledge of program activity and best practices for all sport programs. Thorough knowledge of the athletic equipment manager's association and membership (AEMA) could be mandatory at certain institutions. All ideal candidates should possess the AEMA Certification from the Athletic Equipment Manager's Association; and have knowledge of applicable rules and standards of the conference that the college belongs to, the National Collegiate Athletic Association (NCAA), as well as other associations and agencies to which the institution adheres to in order to avoid any violations of these rules and standards governed by the conference and/or the National Collegiate Athletic Association.

Professional Sport Management

Professional sport management can annually generate billions of dollars; however, this money is not translated to the "behind the scenes" employees who decide to work in the professional sport empire. While the daily expectation of hearing the latest contractual agreement between the sport team and a professional athlete is exciting, the worker bees for these professional teams are not earning lucrative salaries. The individuals who decide to pursue a higher level of sport management in professional sport will play an important role in providing high-quality sport entertainment for customers and fans, regardless of the annual salary for that position. Professional sport teams are business organizations that have a vast history of providing an environment that values the needs of the people via entertainment. Throughout the past several decades, the need to improve diversity and reach out internationally has provided additional opportunities for personal challenge, growth, and pride. All employees, including non-athletes, are professionals dedicated to providing a service and should be passionate about delivering a quality product to their guests and clients.

There are many jobs and positions available for kinesiology sport management students in the realm of professional sport, may this be with organizations in the NFL, NBA, MLB, NHL, or other professional leagues overseas. These jobs listed below are very similar in responsibilities and qualifications at the intercollegiate athletic level. The only exception is working behind the scenes with the business side of the sport compared to working directly or indirectly with student-athletes and coaches.

1. Administrative Positions
2. Marketing/Promotions/Sales
3. Facility Operations
4. Equipment Management
5. Communications
6. Media/Internet
7. Community Relations

Many of these main career opportunities have already been addressed that piggy-back on intercollegiate athletics positions. There are also other opportunities not listed in this chapter but available as a career in professional sport that would lead to a successful profession.

Essential Qualities and Responsibilities for Professional Sport Staff

The following qualities and responsibilities are needed in order for you to pursue and advance at the level of a professional sport management career:

- Ability to interact positively with large fan base
- Must be detail oriented and have strong organizational skills
- Strong interpersonal and verbal communication skills
- Strong sales skills; background in sales or marketing is strongly encouraged
- Ability to work in a fast-paced environment and use problem-solving skills
- Must be willing to work nights, weekends, and holidays, if necessary
- Must be able to work in a variety of weather conditions
- Must be able to stand for long periods of time and walk long distances in parking lots and stadium complex
- All candidates may be subject to background checks and drug testing

While a degree in kinesiology-sport management carries some credence for those looking at professional teams, hiring recruiters are more interested in seeing experience through internships and working in collegiate environments. Many teams are also partial to former college athletes, especially in sales roles. Selling requires mental toughness and an ability to overcome obstacles. These are qualities often associated with competitive athletes. Also, between traveling and various starting times for games, this will not be a regular working environment.

Here is the good news regarding professional sport. Regardless of a bumpy economy, the sport industry is thriving constantly. This means many professional teams are hiring even as other sectors of the economy cut back. The job outlook for professional sport is very good with regards to entry-level positions. The challenge will be the lower starting salary and rough competition. If you can sell lots of tickets and team merchandise through individual or group sales, you will move up quickly in this cutthroat industry.

CHAPTER 9
Corporate Wellness

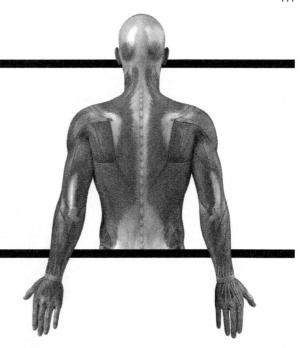

A few years ago when I was discussing kinesiology careers, the topic of corporate wellness was brought up as a viable option for kinesiology majors. The topic ensued on how one qualifies a worksite as having a corporate wellness program. One student raised a hand and said her parents had been given discount coupons to join a local gym through their employer and asked if that counted. I admit there is much confusion when describing a corporate wellness program. This chapter will help define this concept as well as provide insight to the potential jobs available, qualifications, and if this fits your current interest as a potential career path in the kinesiology field.

When someone mentions the term "corporate," it usually refers to the business culture of an industry. When you add the term "wellness," this could confuse many to decide what kind of career path this title would evoke. In the field of kinesiology, would this suggest a combination of both the physiological exercise science subdiscipline combined with the sport management subdiscipline side of kinesiology? I would agree based on my own experiences as a former corporate fitness intern at General Dynamics and a former Southern California Regional Corporate Fitness coordinator for the now-defunct First Interstate Bancorp that is now Wells Fargo Bank. Corporate wellness is an onsite wellness program designed to promote healthy behavior at the worksite and to improve the health status of employees. A corporate wellness program should provide a variety of activities such as on-site fitness programs, annual health fairs, stress management seminars, health screenings, wellness coaching, weight management programs, monthly wellness newsletters, smoking cessation, and additional educational programs. Corporate wellness programs include organizational policies allowing employee health practices during working hours such as allowing flex time for workouts, providing on-site eating and cooking facilities, offering healthy food options at cafes or vending machines, "walking and talking" meetings, and financial incentives for participating or accomplishing set wellness goals such as reducing smoking or calorie intake. Corporate wellness programs have improved over the past decade to include all facets of health at the worksite.

Figure 9.1: The Wellness Wheel

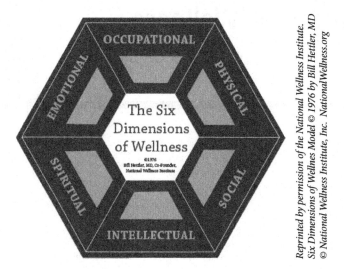

The Six Dimensions of Wellness

In order to describe the concept of "wellness" and differentiate this term from "fitness," the six dimensions of wellness must be explained in detail (Figure 9.1). The Six Dimensional Wellness Model was originally developed by Dr. Bill Hettler, a cofounder of the National Wellness Institute. This interdependent figure depicting six areas provides the ultimate conceptual framework from which "wellness" is defined. The six interdependent areas of wellness are social, occupational, spiritual, physical, intellectual, and emotional wellness. Let's start explaining these six dimensions of wellness with the first one listed, social wellness.

Social Wellness

The social wellness dimension encourages contributing to improving your interpersonal relationships, understanding and developing friendships, and building a better self through understanding yourself as well as others. Getting to know and appreciate others for who they are and what they represent is part of socialization. I believe we all will agree that in a perfect world, wouldn't it be nice to have minimal conflict with others and basically just get along? This category emphasizes the interdependence between you and others you decide to relate and communicate with. Learning to be at peace with yourself and reducing strife in your life does improve your overall health and disposition. No one really wants to be grumpy, angry, or apathetic to the point where you cannot get along with your neighbors, co-workers, or your boss or supervisor. The way you promote and exist is important to society as well as the impact you have on multiple social levels within your environment. By taking steps to improve your communication skills will help encourage healthier living by initiating better communication. Those who actively seek ways to promote balance within nature discover how powerful these choices relate towards enhancing personal relationships and friendships, and build a healthier life in the long run towards positive interactions with others.

Occupational Wellness

The occupational wellness dimension encourages personal development and satisfaction in life through the process of one's occupation or worksite. If you can visualize the math, an average person will spend at least one-third or greater of his or her life at a worksite or performing a task to maintain a form of livelihood. It's very rare that you will meet a person who doesn't work to make ends meet, or if the person is financially well off, having an internal satisfaction of accomplishing tasks does play an important role with self-satisfaction and total life happiness for all human beings. At the center of occupational wellness is the premise that occupational development is related to one's attitude about one's work. Traveling a path toward your occupational wellness, there is an expectation for everyone to contribute their skills, desires, and talents at an occupation that is both personally rewarding and satisfying. Hopefully, the choice of a kinesiology profession, job satisfaction, career ambitions, and personal accomplishments are all important attributes toward finding overall happiness and staying healthy for the rest of your life.

Spiritual Wellness

The spiritual wellness dimension involves one's search for the meaning or purpose towards life. What is it that you represent or what you want to believe in? Spirituality can include belonging or practicing a certain religion but one does not have to belong to a religious entity in order to be spiritual. It does involve a deep appreciation for the purpose of living life and how one fits into the sequence of your universe. Many religions or philosophies seek the existence of finding internal peace and harmony between internal personal feelings and emotions. Everyone goes through a path of acknowledgement of why you exist and what your purpose in life should be. Feelings of doubt, possibly the fear of the unknown, experiencing disappointment, or being disillusioned with your current phase vs. feelings of pleasure, joy, happiness, and seeking virtue are all important experiences everyone goes through at several points in their personal life. Seeking answers to your questions about your existence and what you represent and what others know about you are part of finding yourself through the path of spirituality. A corporate wellness program should have activities that promote and find opportunities for people to discover what they are and what they want to become while traveling down the road called life. Opportunities to discover the meaning of life and what can bring internal peace, or what Abraham Maslow calls "self-actualization," becomes a journey many choose not to pursue but is as important as the other dimensions of wellness.

Physical Wellness

The physical wellness dimension becomes the most obvious category of the six dimensions with regards to participating in physical activity.   Besides focusing on the fitness development and maintenance, the area also encourages learning about proper nutrition and reduction in the use of drugs and tobacco products. Corporate fitness programs focus on this primary area as the "meat and potatoes" offerings to employees. When considering the physical wellness component, there are five distinct areas that should be addressed. A comprehensive fitness program should include muscular strength, muscular endurance, flexibility, body composition, and cardiorespiratory fitness. After filling out a health appraisal and an informed consent permission form, the exercise specialist should perform a battery of tests to assess the five areas of fitness. Once these results have been tabulated, your fitness goals should be combined to set up an exercise prescription to address your weaknesses and maintain your strengths. An orientation of the types of exercises should follow so the employee is comfortable about the designed prescription and when to make amendments to this program. Regular assessments should be offered to the employees every four to six weeks to determine improvements and adjustments to the existing routine. Many group exercise classes are offered at corporate wellness programs to assist with not only the physical dimension of wellness but with other areas as well. Education on the responsibility and care for minor athletic injuries should be addressed with the employees as well as an understanding of basic first aid and CPR at the workplace.

Intellectual Wellness

The intellectual wellness dimension characterizes the ability to stimulate your brain through cognitive activities. The use and continued challenge to improve one's knowledge and mental skill is extremely important for mental health. The cliché, "Use it or lose it," has been correlated not just with skeletal muscles but also with brain cells. We, as human beings, need to be challenged in order to adapt. Using intellectual and cognitive activities at the worksite and through learning resources available within the corporate wellness center, employees will cherish the ability to promote intellectual growth and stimulation. This particular wellness path, in conjunction with other wellness dimensions, could foster the ability to problem solve, enhance creativity, and increase learning. As one ages, it is very important to maintain cognitive skills and constantly work on being challenged. If your job or tasks you perform aren't allowing this to occur, having a corporate wellness program can prove invaluable worth. The activities are beyond reading books, magazines, or surfing the Internet for stories or new ideas to stimulate your brain. Fostering the environment towards developing your intellectual curiosity will allow one to make positive gains to expand and challenge your mind without having to seek this out elsewhere but at work.

Emotional Wellness

The emotional wellness dimension recognizes how people relate to their environment through their feelings. Emotional wellness includes the scope of how individuals feel about themselves may it be a tide of emotions ranging from being happy to pure sadness. It includes the ability to manage your own feelings and behaviors, especially under the duress of stress. The ability to manage stress also falls in this wellness category. Many employees suffer from stress-related issues at work as well as daily stressors from their home life to personal conflicts. A healthy person can maintain positive and productive relationships with others. Having the ability to accept your own feelings and being aware of what is normal compared to unhealthy is promoting good health practices. Once you are connected to being on the wellness path, the ability to express feelings freely and productively without harming others or yourself can lead to great accomplishments in life. Not just within the corporate or company environment, being independent and showing empathy also go a long way toward seeking and appreciating the support and assistance of others. Forming interdependent relationships with others at work as well as in your personal life can help develop a foundation for mutual respect, trust, and overall emotional security. Over time, you will be able to accept challenges, take risks, and recognize conflict as being potentially healthy. A corporate wellness program should provide programs that enhance the emotional dimension of employees in order to allow healthy outcomes to be part of a comprehensive curriculum at the workplace.

Rationale of Implementing Corporate Wellness

Historically, corporate wellness programs have proven their worth regardless of the upfront costs associated with starting and continuing these programs that are provided by the company as a benefit for the employees. Of course, it would also benefit the company based on the outcomes which will be explained further into this description. So then, doesn't every employee want to participate? Just because the outcomes would greatly benefit individuals, some people just choose not to partake or do not want to lead a healthy lifestyle. Sometimes, any activity or wellness program associated with the concept of employment becomes a negative factor for those who are just unhappy or unmotivated to be productive employees. Human beings can be unpredictable creatures. You have heard the cliché that you can lead a horse to water but you cannot make it drink. All of these wellness programs are considered long-term investments. In a society where many people want to be rewarded instantly, it takes work to lose a few inches off the waistline or to reduce one's resting blood pressure. These changes do not happen overnight or within a week of participating in a wellness program at work. Due to this concept, there will be people who would rather take chances on quick fixes or non-proven cures that guarantee results in a short period of time. Education is the key to modifying one's behavior and having the right kind of program and staff to facilitate these behavior changes at the worksite. I was taught early on in my health promotion classes that behavioral change theories are plentiful, however, unpredictable on the human species. It is very difficult to change one's behavior, especially after adolescent years. Yes, you can teach an old dog new tricks but the old dog has to buy into the behavioral changes, not because a wellness coach or wellness specialist gives this dog the magic bone. It is because this old dog has totally bought into the new trick and allows the positive changes to occur.

With regards to the company or corporation itself, there is the major investment of money and time in order to improve the health of its employees. It is not cheap or productive to cut corners on developing and initiating a corporate wellness program for employees. It is extremely costly to hire qualified corporate wellness employees, meaning that the staff would encompass the six dimensions of wellness. Many CEOs of large firms will acknowledge that a healthier group of employees will benefit their company as well as the employees of the company. According to the Wellness Council of America, a national organization consisting of over 500 members representing corporations or companies nationwide, if a business develops a fully encompassed wellness program consisting of the six wellness dimensions, the following could result from the participation of the company employees:

- A company could gain an average of $5.81 for every dollar invested in corporate wellness programs.
- A well-managed corporate wellness program can reduce sick-leave absenteeism by 27%.
- Corporate wellness programs can reduce healthcare costs by 26%.
- The results of a well-run corporate wellness program could reduce worker's compensation and disability claims up to 32%.

Additional Advantages to Corporate Wellness Programs

The company employees can reap the six dimensions of wellness benefits as described earlier in the chapter reading by participating in a company-sponsored wellness program. The Principal Financial Group, an international financial organization, provided a nationwide survey to American workers canned the "Well-being Index for American Workers." Based on the findings, American workers viewed themselves much more physically fit (57%) than financially fit (28%), although the employees conceptualized that maintaining physical activity and good overall wellness is an investment toward their financial future. It is interesting to note that most Americans will agree about the importance of wellness, even at the workplace. Other key findings from the 2014 survey included the following:

- The vast majority of American workers (84%) recognized maintaining a physical wellness dimension is an investment in their financial future.
- Nearly half of American workers (46%) felt stressed about their current financial status and this affected not only their emotional wellness but how they performed at the workplace.

American workers who are practicing wellness based on the six dimensions of wellness start their workday with more energy and motivation. Here are more facts based from the survey:

- 51% of American workers state they work harder and perform better after exercise.
- 59% of American workers state they have more energy and are more productive at work and at home after exercise.
- 45% of American workers believe their health benefits program encourages them to stay in their current position and company.
- 43% of American workers are not taking sick leave as a result of the corporate wellness programs.

Figure 9.2:

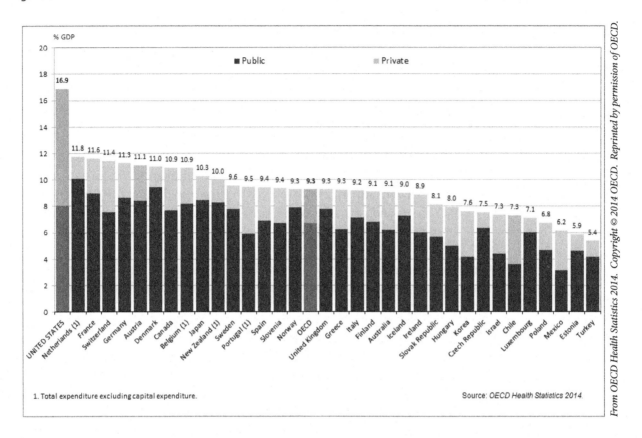

The Corporate Wellnesss Specialist

After reading the benefits of a sponsored corporate wellness program by the company and the workers, why do you think only 34% of company employees still decide to decline these benefits? Why are these workers deciding not to participate in company-sponsored wellness program? Once again, human beings will be human beings and this concept was discussed earlier in the chapter. It will be up to you, if you decide to advance your career as a corporate wellness specialist to tackle these concerns and offer strategies that can be very effective at the worksite, such as offering incentives and inserting other mechanisms that will convince the other 66% that participating in these programs is a no-brainer. Additional coursework in your kinesiology classes as well as advice from your academic advisor to take additional courses in either psychology or business will help you toward selling the program to those who refuse to participate in a wonderful opportunity to live their life more completely and lead to a fuller satisfaction of their self as an employee at a company that demonstrates care for its workers. Figure 9.2 indicates that the United States spends the most amount of money on healthcare. That amount is not only coming from the companies that support health benefit programs for their employees, it also is coming from taxpayers, meaning you and me as well as the people who are spending money on medical treatment vs. focusing the attention on prevention, such as a company-sponsored wellness program. It will be your task besides supporting a company wellness program to tackle the majority of workers who still are not sold on the importance of corporate wellness at their worksite.

Important Qualities of a Corporate Wellness Specialist

1. **Self-motivated.** Corporate wellness specialists are left by themselves in most work environments. There are opportunities to multitask—from preparing the facility in the early mornings, teaching classes, answering phones and making appointments, to assessing fitness and prescriptions, and meeting and greeting members—are all within a day's work. You are the leader of the worksite during most days and it's important to understand you are responsible for the safety of all participants who are choosing to give an average of an hour of their personal time to reap these wonderful benefits you are providing for them at the wellness center. To provide the best experience to all members, you need to use your time wisely and be attentive to the members at all stages of their visit.

2. **Team Player.** Even though you will be on your own for a period of time, you are part of the wellness team and a company employee when servicing the members, from motivating them to come into the wellness center to encouraging them to return the next day. Everyone who is an employee has to fully understand their role for the company and towards working with each other to maintain professionalism and organization within the corporate wellness program. Being able to cover for another employee when an emergency arises to being able to take care of members during the heavy use hours with a smile on your face is very important to the philosophy of wellness promotion. Supporting each other by helping another wellness specialist will go a long way towards supporting the six dimensions of wellness by demonstrating this in front of others.

3. **Problem Solver.** Within any corporate wellness or facility, things will go wrong, from missing payroll deduction forms to misplaced fitness programs and membership files. It was common back in my days as an exercise specialist at the First Interstate Bank for the soap dispenser to break or the showers to develop a broken handle. In these instances, you must act as the public relations manager working on behalf of the company and wellness program to quickly and expeditiously take care of the problems. Even though you are a corporate wellness employee, part of your role is customer service to the worksite employees. It is very similar to working in the food or hotel industry. Pleasing the customers is also an important facet when you want these employees to come

back regularly. They won't come back if the showers are always broken or the dysfunctional treadmill is not fixed within 48 hours. Whether the episode is making your job harder or not, it's not okay to let members see your frustrations publicly. Be resourceful and make the best of the situation. You won't always agree with what's happening to something that's out of your control. It's difficult not to revert to member mentality and side with the folks staring at you, but remember your role and put that smile on your face and take responsibility and let the members know everything has been taken care of and follow through on your claims.

4.   **Extroverted Positive Cheerleader.** So, you are a team player, self-motivated, and can solve problems as they appear out of nowhere. You are going to be a non-factor within a corporate wellness program unless you are also the public cheerleader and a daily wellness coach. I have had students who I had to convince that corporate wellness would not be a good fit for their kinesiology career based on their personality. It is true you cannot change one's personality since this is innate but you can change behavior. When you become a corporate wellness employee, you have to be an extrovert when you arrive on the premises, to the time you leave the parking lot. Introverts or those who cannot greet members who come in at 5 a.m. with a scowl on their face because they haven't had their endorphin kick or their caffeine boost will be ineffective towards winning these candidates over. You will be teaching group fitness classes or giving small to moderate size class lectures on a health or wellness related topic. You must put on your Tony Robbins hat and become the politician or salesperson and sell your product to the membership of employees who need your pep talk to encourage or change behavior and make the effort to embrace the six dimensions of wellness. Selling is a large part of the job in corporate wellness and even though you will not be on a commission-based salary, the ability to change people's behaviors and see the results should be altruistic enough for anyone to receive instead.

5.   **Effective.** Can you arrive to a corporate wellness program and create outcomes within the employee membership who are expecting to see results from your efforts? Okay, physical fitness workouts need to be effective but do they really need to be difficult to get results? Education is the key to becoming effective with the employees within an employee-based wellness program. Is your communication style pleasant and motivating without being harsh or disrespectful? Be clear in your expectations among participants where they are versus where you think they should be. If they fail to reach their goals based on poor behavior on their part, what methods can be implemented to revitalize their energies to get their goals which could lead to positive reinforcement to continue with these new behaviors? Being an effective educator and communicator are key to changing health behaviors without being punitive and ineffective.

Job Duties of a Corporate Wellness Specialist

There are different roles and duties when running or working for a corporate wellness program, depending upon the company's philosophy and management structure. There will be companies that strictly focus on the physical wellness dimension when advertising for a wellness coordinator or supervisor. Regardless, the hope continues that any candidate will be able to sell or implement all six dimensions of wellness without incurring additional costs upon the company or corporation. Regardless of the missing pieces of a corporate wellness program, the wellness or fitness coordinator will be responsible for overseeing the day-to-day operations of the fitness/wellness center along with the planning, coordination, delivery, tracking, and reporting of physical activity programs. This position is responsible for providing outstanding service to members and program participants to maximize participation, outcomes, and customer satisfaction. Here are other duties that are expected at most company sites:

1. Supervises the wellness center operations on a continuous basis; assists with the supervision of classes as necessary
2. Effectively communicates proper training and exercise techniques as well as safety regulations to all employee participants
3. Assists the program director in the delivery of wellness materials, including monthly or bimonthly newsletters and brochures
4. Attends all required training sessions and scheduled meetings with corporate board of directors
5. Remains available to all participants to answer questions, review class instruction/materials, and review fitness testing procedures; greets new participants and assists in program development
6. Actively promotes safety protocols to include warmup, cooldown, training intensities, heart rate monitoring, and other routines as appropriate; holds current first aid/CPR/AED certifications
7. Assists with wellness-related special events as requested
8. Assists in the coordination, promotion, and implementation of fitness testing and protocols
9. Proactively builds relationships among employees to seek and retain memberships
10. Creates weekly and monthly facilities and equipment checklists for maintenance and repair protocols
11. Manages day-to-day operations of the wellness center including customer service, cleanliness, and equipment maintenance
12. Tracks participation and outcomes and celebrates employee success stories

An entry-level salary for a corporate wellness specialist is between $26,000 and $28,000 nationally. Those who enter middle management with a master's degree are in the mid to high $40,000 range, depending upon the company's structure and the size of the company.

Corporate Wellness Specialist Training, CEUs, Degree, License, Advancement

A four-year degree in kinesiology or health promotion–based curriculum is required even though degrees in recreation have been accepted in the past. Many high-level corporate wellness programs will hire those who have specific curriculum and internship experience in corporate wellness. It would be highly suggestive that taking a few business courses or even minoring in sport management or business would be a definite plus with regards to administrative tasks associated with running a wellness program at the corporate level. Besides the bachelor's degree, a background or experience in developing health or wellness strategies is preferred for entry-level positions. Most candidates must have the ability to teach group classes, may they be lecture or physical activity. Developing new programs that keep up with fitness trends and promoting the six dimensions of wellness are a definite plus for candidates who are attempting to separate themselves from the field of applicants.

Supervisor or mid-management in corporate wellness will need a master's degree in either kinesiology or sport management/business along with a minimum of five years of full-time experience managing health or wellness programs. Another requirement will be the familiarity with vendors who service the corporate wellness industry (fitness equipment, repair facilities, medical contacts, etc.). Possessing excellent oral, written, and presentation skills as well as the ability to demonstrate the success of customer service and team building skills to motivate staff, clients, and report to upper management to figures needed to justify that corporate wellness is being effective within the corporation.

CHAPTER 10
Early Career Do's or Don'ts

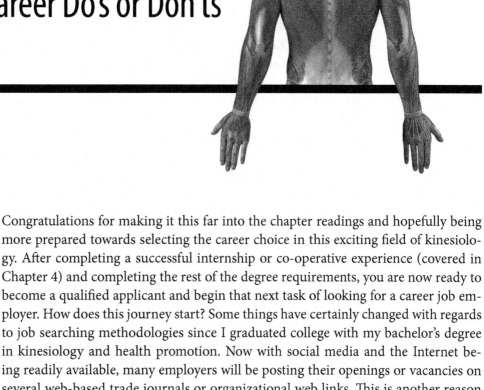

Congratulations for making it this far into the chapter readings and hopefully being more prepared towards selecting the career choice in this exciting field of kinesiology. After completing a successful internship or co-operative experience (covered in Chapter 4) and completing the rest of the degree requirements, you are now ready to become a qualified applicant and begin that next task of looking for a career job employer. How does this journey start? Some things have certainly changed with regards to job searching methodologies since I graduated college with my bachelor's degree in kinesiology and health promotion. Now with social media and the Internet being readily available, many employers will be posting their openings or vacancies on several web-based trade journals or organizational web links. This is another reason why it is so important to belong to certain professional organizations, as discussed in Chapter 4. Not just being a student member of a professional career organization opens the door, attending their regional and national conferences gets a foot in the door since this will allow you to see job openings being advertised at the conference locations. Many of these representatives are actually physically there at the conference, waiting for candidates to contact them for on-site interviews. This gives you an extra advantage since many applicants do not get to meet anyone when they apply online or through the snail mail delivery system.

What job finding technique that hasn't changed with finding entry-level positions in kinesiology is the old-fashion method called "word of mouth." The delivery or "mouth" could be through an email, text message, or on a social media message, but this method is still very effective since I use this constantly as I have in the past. My first job in corporate wellness was discovered when my advisor, Dr. Emery, had a chance meeting with me after I graduated with my bachelor's degree. She asked me what my plans were since I just returned from a summer job running a swim camp in Big Bear,

California. I told her I had several applications out and an upcoming phone interview from another company but if I couldn't find anything within the next month, I would consider returning back to earn my master's degree. She said a classmate of mine received a promotion to a managerial position with the First Interstate Bancorp in Los Angeles and that he was looking for an applicant to fill his previous position. I quickly ran to the nearest pay phone (another concept that doesn't happen these days due to everyone having a cell phone) and called to make an appointment for an interview. To make a long story short, two weeks later I was chosen for the position as an exercise specialist for the First Interstate Bancorp and started my career as a corporate wellness specialist in downtown Los Angeles. In retrospect, did it help that we both had commonalities? The answer is "yes." Did it also help that I had a great internship experience at General Dynamics, a major defense contractor that employed over 10,000 employees? The answer is "yes." Did it make a major difference that my mentor and faculty advisor assisted in convincing this classmate that I would be a great fit? That answer is "absolutely." So, when I hear from students and colleagues that "it's who you know and not what you know," I believe this is totally a bogus statement. Did I know that classmate who interviewed me for this entry-level corporate wellness position? That answer is "yes." Did it help that he also had a lot of respect and admiration for my faculty advisor, Dr. Lynne Emery? That answer also becomes a "yes." Did I get the job based on these connections? That answer is "no." I was fully qualified for the position based on my academic preparation, my past experience performing corporate wellness during a successful internship, and my ability to have certain characteristics that became a good fit (see Chapter 9) for improving the existing program at the First Interstate Bancorp. I caution anyone who still believes this is how one gets a position is by "who you know." I fully believe it's a combination of both. It is "who you know" and also "what you know" that provide you the opportunity to earn the position.

You Earned the Job, Now What?!

I remember getting my very first official paystub after the first two weeks of being on the job. I was thinking I was going to celebrate and splurge with my friends that weekend. Since I was making the "big bucks" for the first time in my life, I thought dinner and drinks would be my treat. That thought quickly changed after looking at the figures on the paystub for the very first time. I had no understanding or concept about certain deductions affecting my paycheck. When I was working part time as an undergraduate, due to the low amounts I was making and my part-time status, benefits and the nature of deductions did not affect my amount nor did it affect my thinking towards educating me on these types of deductions. When you get your first real job, even though someone in either the payroll or human resources department gives you the brief discussion on deductions and benefits, your thought process is not focused on these issues due to the excitement of being hired for the very first time in a real career opportunity. This was how I felt along with many others who go through this phenomenon that I call "paycheck bliss." You are finally making a whole lot more money than you have before and most likely this is your first time working a real job in your career field. How exciting is this for any person to experience? But due to the distractions of certain feelings or being giddy due to this short-term excitement, your pragmatic financial side of the brain reworks the stimulus back to your dopamine producers. The pleasure of knowing you will be making more money for the first time in your life tends to block the ability to ask pertinent questions like, "After these benefits and deductions, what would my take-home pay be after the pay period?" I had to find out the hard way after the first pay period by looking at my check amount in shock, then looking at the deductions taken out and wondering what happened to all the money I earned during this pay period.

Let us talk about the important questions you need to ask once you have been hired by a firm or company as a full-time employee that sometimes escape us since the adrenalin pump has been flowing in cycles, causing the ability to forget about asking them. These important questions include:

1. Are the pay periods weekly, bimonthly, or monthly?
2. What benefits are fully covered by the company or employers (i.e., medical, dental, optical, life insurance, disability, long-term care, investments or pension plans for retirement)?
3. What deductions are standard deductions (Social Security tax, federal tax, state tax, local tax, Medicare tax, and other benefits that are standard such as Affordable Care, retirement)?
4. How many sick days, vacation days, personal days, etc. am I allowed and does this increase once I reach a certain time period?
5. Is there a probation period in my employment contract and what constitutes being terminated before this period is over?
6. How often does a review period lead into a salary adjustment or a raise in salary? Is it every six months or annually? Can an adjustment occur after a probationary period?
7. If you are a salary worker, what are the expectations that working over 40 hours/week will be the expectation and if you are on an hourly pay scale, if overtime pay is permitted after exceeding 40 hours per week?

Back in high school and even in college course, I was given the background and knowledge to set up and develop a household budget. I failed miserably at performing this task when I got my first real job. The excitement prevented me from realizing this important task and I actually overspent money I did not have the very first month of being on the job due to being underprepared for realizing that even though I was not a starving college student anymore, I was on the verge of being a broke professional by overspending and not being fiscally responsible.

Figure 10.1: Sample Pay Stub

Kinesiology Employer.
450 Healthy Street
Somewhere in California, USA 01010

Employee Name: John Smith
Social Security #: 999-99-9999
Period End Date: 01/07/15

Wages					**Deductions**		
Description	Hours	Rate	Current Amount	Y-T-D Amount	Description	Current Amount	Y-T-D Amount
Regular	40.00	10.00	400.00	400.00	Federal Withholdings	37.29	37.29
Overtime	1.00	15.00	15.00	15.00	Social Security Tax	24.83	24.83
Holiday				0.00	Medicare	5.81	5.81
Tuition			37.43*	37.43	Tax	8.26	8.26
					CA State	5.11	5.11
					Income Tax	0.61	0.61
					CA State Income Tax		
					CA SUI/SDI Tax		
					Other		
					401(k)	27.15*	27.15
					Life Insurance	2.00	2.00
					Loan	30.00	30.00
					Dental	2.00*	2.00
					HMO	20.00*	20.00
					Depend. Care FSA	30.00*	30.00
Totals			452.43	452.43	**Deduction Totals**	193.06	193.06
Taxable Gross			335.85	335.85	**NET PAY**	259.38	259.38

After viewing the sample pay stub (Figure 10.1), you may understand how confusing your net pay differs from the gross amount that many people are expecting as their paycheck. I learned this lesson the hard way and had to make adjustments to my lifestyle in order to accommodate the investments toward my future. This meant taking advantage of my health benefits by using the providers I was paying for towards promoting my overall wellness through preventive means. That meant visiting a dentist, an optometrist, physician, etc. even though I was feeling healthy and thought there were no immediate issues. I would have not used my benefits in the past even though I was paying for this, just due to the notion that I was a healthy individual and the only time anyone should visit a medical practitioner is if you were ill. We all should practice what we preach and focus on the preventive methods vs. ending up paying the extra money when we really need medical treatments. I ended up getting a prescription for my eyes, cleaning for dental, and a follow-up on my skin from years of lifeguarding and teaching swimming without using any sun block or additional protection. I tended to see other young professionals who are entering their first career job go through similar feelings of wellness neglect, especially when they were being provided benefits.

Please take advantage of these deductions and use them to your advantage before you run the risk of finding out that your neglect precipitated a condition to become worse.

Do I really need all that student loan money to fund my education?

According to the 2011 U.S. News and Report, Americans owed over $870 billion in student loan debt which surpasses the amount of debt in credit cards in this country. Delinquencies are extremely high with student loans compared to regular household debt and the numbers are growing to 25% of students being unable to keep up with their payment schedules. The majority of these borrowers are over the age of 30 but there are people in their 60s and 70s still paying off student loans today.

I am not against taking out student loans. For many students, this is a necessity in order to attend school and earn a four-year degree. I am a product of borrowing money from the federal government and without the assistance from student loans I would have struggled to complete my studies in a reasonable amount of time. But based on my own observations and experience, it is highly abused by college students and not taken seriously towards the goal of repaying them off, once you have completed your studies. I had college roommates who used their student loan money to buy stereo systems for their dorm rooms, purchase tires for their car, or take spring break trips with the money that was earmarked towards paying for books, supplies, and tuition. I agree it is easier to make the assumptions that once you graduate, you will get a great paying job and you had intent to pay off your student loan debt. Unfortunately, the latest statistics are showing very high levels of default. Default occurs when you are unable or unwilling to submit a payment after 270 days of the billing due date. New legislation now prevents student loan defaulters from any form of credit history forgiveness as bankruptcy provides after seven years. The following may result once you go into default for your student loans:

- You may be turned down for future credit cards, auto or home loans, or rental agreements.
- Your interest rate could rise on your existing loans and credit cards.
- Lending institutions may refuse to allow you to open a savings or checking account.
- You might be charged a higher premium on your insurance.
- You could be denied a renewal on a professional license.
- Employers perform credit checks during hiring phases which would result in losing a potential job.

Borrow only what you truly need and withhold the gratification of spending your student loan money on extras that can wait when you do get your first entry-level kinesiology position. Also, since we brought up the concept of understanding your paycheck, you should wisely consider setting up a monthly budget to pay down your loan while saving towards items that will help increase your overall wellness such as a home or automobile. I have seen fellow colleagues who earn a great income but have taken out over $100,000 in student loans. It makes your life tougher to pay this debt off when you should be enjoying what your education provided. Look at your future and make this decision wisely about the amount you really need to borrow. I was able to pay off my loans within seven years but I never paid the minimum. When this occurs, you just pay interest and not the principal. Paying down the principal helps with paying less interest over the life of the loan. The good news is that paying on time and on a regular cycle builds great credit history and assists you with larger purchases that many people want eventually, such as a house. If you have problems paying your student loan payments, do not wait for default to occur. Contact your lender immediately and work out a plan to make lower payments. Does this create more added interest to your principal balance? Yes, but you save your credit history and you spare the issues of dealing with collection agencies and other forms of aggravations listed above. Be smart and borrow sparingly.

Goal Setting for the Immediate Future

Within the first week or month on the job, there will be young professionals who start to forget about looking towards the future and within several years, they are running into a quagmire, an unfortunate situation where they have lost the advantage of having momentum on their side towards fielding or parlaying into the next phase of their career. Within the very first month of being at my new entry-level corporate wellness job at the First Interstate Bancorp, I already had my eyes set on applying for graduate school in kinesiology. At the time, I didn't know what true advantages I would receive with a master's degree in kinesiology but I was banking (no pun intended) on future opportunities that would magically appear if I kept plugging away at investing into my future, even though I was pretty happy and satisfied with my current employment outlook. Refer to Chapter 3 with regards to the description and laboratory that was associated with this important point towards achieving career success. Many people who enter the workforce for the very first time (and I am generalizing with this statement) lose their momentum and forget about the next step on their pyramid to achieving their ultimate career goal (Figure 10.2). I was very fortunate that I knew I wanted to work my way up the pyramid but never had an opportunity to plan it the way I now highly suggest through this textbook.

Figure 10.2: Goal Setting Pyramid to Career Success

Graduate School: Is This for Everyone?

Recently I overheard a conversation between someone in the kinesiology field and another colleague regarding the reasons why he was not moving up the corporate ladder. The conversation was based on his inability to get to the next level compared to another co-worker who was given a promotion over him. "Yeah, I should have gone to back graduate school 10 years ago when I had the chance" was his reply that I overheard from his conversation. I quickly thought if his rationale was that simple, he probably wasn't the only person who felt that obtaining a graduate degree is that feasible to obtain.

Thirty years ago, the percentage of Americans who possessed a four-year degree was less than 20%. Currently, more than 30% (35% for women and 27% for men) of Americans have earned bachelor's degrees, the highest percentage in our nation's history; minorities have more access to higher education; and women are the gender group that has surpassed their male counterpart over the past decade. Based on this fact, the competition for getting certain jobs in the field of kinesiology has been raised. So, the scenario of applying for a job comes down to the experience and educational level of the candidates. The candidates with a graduate degree will have an advantage over those who only possess a four-year degree. When setting up proper goals within the career pyramid lab, it's also important to understand that not everyone with a four-year degree is accepted into a graduate program. As a graduate coordinator of an existing kinesiology program, I have turned applicants away based on their undergraduate GPA, letter of recommendations, or low Graduate Record Examination (GRE) scores. Also, an essay stating the reasons for selecting the graduate program and what they would accomplish also plays a role towards selecting candidates into a graduate program.

As an example of how these prerequisites can affect your graduate school status, I remember several years back I had a recent four-year graduate who wanted to visit with me about her denial into the kinesiology graduate program. Her undergraduate GPA was a 2.25, the three letters of recommendation were not from academic professors or professional sources, and her GRE scores were way below the acceptable levels of our program requirements. Her claim was that she needed a master's degree in kinesiology to heighten her chances of being considered for a college coaching position and that she has turned over a "new leaf" with regards to her seriousness of being a quality student. She stated her low undergraduate GPA was based on three years of partying, poor mentoring from classmates, and not attending many of her classes. She said she could not find a professor to write her a letter of recommendation based on her academic record and lack of faculty interest in her. I then asked her, "If this is true and you learned a lesson and could turn over a "new leaf" in our graduate program, why did you score low on the Graduate Record Examination?" It seemed she really wasn't ready to turn over a "new leaf" and those are not the kind of students I really want representing our graduate program. As I stated before, not everyone is entitled to go on and qualify for a graduate program in kinesiology. You really have to earn the right and in order to be in the driver's seat, know that the standards will be elevated compared to your undergraduate requirements.

Based on the bar being raised towards being accepted into a graduate program, it is best to play it safe by accomplishing the following tasks as an undergraduate to raise your chance of being accepted if and when you decide a graduate degree in kinesiology would assist towards accomplishing your career goals in this field.

1. Maintain or elevate your overall GPA above a 2.75 by the time you graduate.
2. Make a good impression with several professors in the kinesiology field who would be called upon to write you a letter of recommendation towards your application into a graduate program, especially in classes taught by these educators.
3. Look at other graduate programs and compare the curriculum, requirements, and overall costs.
4. Visit the graduate coordinator and faculty of possible grad programs to see if your needs fit what they are offering.
5. Ask about recent graduates from their graduate program and their career success stories.
6. Does the graduate program you are interested in offer graduate assistantships? Many GAs will waive tuition, fees, and could offer a stipend or the ability to gain additional experience by teaching or performing research for their program.

7. Take the Graduate Records Examination right after you graduate if you think you might apply for graduate school within the next two or three years. That way, the information you have is still fresh and allows you to prepare less compared to those who take a few years off and feel rusty with their analytical and verbal skills, therefore reducing your overall anxiety towards this hoop jump.

8. Perform your homework and check to see if a graduate degree in kinesiology is going to further your career goals and open up more possibilities in the near future, based on the degree type and skills developed in graduate school.

9. Does the investment costs in pursuing and obtaining a graduate degree offset and allow your annual income to increase over the next several years, making this a worthwhile task?

10. Consider hybrid or online graduate programs as long as the institution is reputable, accredited, and the faculty teaches full time at this institution.

As I have stated numerous times before, I was never given an opportunity to "plan" my career through a pyramid concept at an opportune time that has been provided for you in this text. However, I always knew that my first career job would not be my last job, the growth of corporate wellness would be limited with regards to upward mobility within the corporation, qualifying for and being in a graduate program in kinesiology would be a wise investment and could open up potential future career opportunities, and belonging to professional organizations and continuing to network within this field would be worth the time and money invested. The next "Do's" to discuss would be the professional networking and obtaining additional experiences that open up more career doors to continue your upward path towards success in the kinesiology field.

Professional Organizations and Career Networking

When I ask entry-level professionals who are not declared members of certain organizations why they don't join or belong to these professional groups, a common complaint is that it costs too much or they feel the money spent towards a professional membership that costs hundreds of dollars annually is not coming back to them as a benefit. I exactly can relate to these feelings since I said the same thing when asked why I did not join any professional organizations for the first three years after becoming a "professional." I ended up joining the American College of Sports Medicine as a professional member during my last year of completing my master's degree due to necessity. The necessity was based on the recommendation coming from my thesis advisor stating it was strongly suggested that I needed to be a member in order to submit my thesis for presentation consideration at their annual conference held once a year at a major city venue. So, I joined ACSM but still I didn't understand what I got for my membership dues besides having to say I was a professional member.

After making a higher salary based either on cost of living adjustments (COLA) or merit pay based on the employer's expectations over the next several years of full-time employment, it became a little easier to join and justify belonging to other professional organizations. But, if you would have asked me what I got for my membership dues, I would not be able to give you a reply and probably would shrug my shoulders as part of my response as would many other members who felt the same way. Apathy does set in since I ran into several colleagues who would quit paying their annual dues because they weren't getting anything back from joining the organization. I finally had my "aha" moment around that career stage that allowed me to see the glass half full vs. half empty and now have different viewpoints I now share with my students and young professionals when it comes to joining and belonging to professional organizations.

How do I get my investment back from professional organizations?

If I join an organization and pay professional dues or membership fees, what do I get for my money? This is a common question asked by potential members regarding any organization that charges membership fees or annual dues. For several years, I could not see what I was receiving back from these organizations that I paid dues to besides a trade or research journal or monthly/quarterly newsletter and the request to attend a conference or meeting at a large metropolitan city. One day, I decided to think about the cliché, "If you can't beat them, join them." I thought about what I wanted to get out of the organization and how I could use this group to push my own agenda and career goals. I decided to become proactive and find a positive way of getting my money back from each organization I belonged to. Here is a synopsis of what I did and how I earned my money back.

1. Run for an elected position on the Board of Directors or for an appointment to be part of the decision-making process of the organization to push your agenda and visibility.
2. Absorb the new and exciting research that interests you to improve your knowledge base to prove you are the expert or being willing to show you have information other colleagues or competitors won't possess by attending the annual meetings or conventions where this information is being presented.
3. Apply for grants or funding prospects offered by several organizations in the kinesiology field that many people will not pursue. Here is another opportunity to get your investment back as well as promote yourself towards your career success.
4. Schedule your vacation time around these conferences or conventions to absorb everything that is going on (i.e., exhibits, lectures on the latest methods, equipment, professional networking).
5. Volunteer for helping during the conference or convention to defray costs or fees associated with attending these events. Conference fees can run $500 or more for certain professional organizations and working a few hours behind the registration booth or providing assistance in other areas could be a way to save hundreds of dollars and provide a valuable service to the organization.

I have learned that being proactive and not whining about why I felt my own personal needs weren't being met is the best approach towards reaching your career goals through a professional organization. I have been fortunate to be part of several boards at the local, state, regional, and national levels. Not only has it helped with my visibility among my peers within the field of kinesiology, but it has also assisted with improving my leadership skills and experience while developing and fostering new friendships and contacts globally. Now, before you start applying for every board position that is available in your current kinesiology organization of specialty, I want to remind you that these potential benefits will take time to develop. Like other life opportunities, several open doors or phone calls go unanswered or unnoticed. Perseverance and tolerance is necessary to maintain one's continued motivation. Do not expect to get your money's worth or investment back within a short time period of starting this process. Eventually, the doors do start to open a little crack at a time. Patience is considered a virtue especially when you can taste the flavor of success after several years of being disappointed.

Professors—Do I really need them after I graduate?

There is not an unwritten rule that says after you graduate and secure a career job in the kinesiology field it is taboo to stay in touch with those professors who made a difference in your academic career. As stated in Chapter 2, mentors or sage mentors could be your former professors or academic advisors who you have connected with in a positive manner. What is the harm in staying in touch with them, unless they have made it perfectly clear they do not want to be bothered by you or anyone else after completing your undergraduate studies at that institution? I am sure there are some professors you choose not to keep in contact with but I believe there are several advantages towards maintaining a professional relationship or friendship with your former professors as was explained in Chapter 2. I have a general rule that I am willing to be a professional or personal reference for former students as long as I stay connected to them once a year. This may be an email update or even a Christmas card or something of that nature, letting me know what they are up to and informing me of their plans. This helps me with the understanding that I can write a letter or answer a reference phone call. Anything longer than a year prevents me from really understanding what they are up to and how my letter or reference can help them with their future goals since I really don't hear or see them anymore.

Before you even list a professor or academic advisor as a reference, you should contact them and ask permission to list them as a professional reference, especially if you are expecting them to be a positive one for you. It seems students or former students take it for granted if they request a professor to become a reference for them, the reference will always be a positive one. That is not always the case so the second rule besides asking permission and keeping annual updates on your work history is to ask,

"If you become a reference check for me, what would be the expectation I could expect from you to a potential employer or company?" If your professor says that most of the information would be positive, would that be your expectation? Honestly, do you exactly know what they would say about you or is it the expectation to receive a "thumbs up" ranking? You need to directly ask your potential reference even though it might feel uncomfortable for your own peace of mind. This reminds me of an incident of a former undergraduate student of mine who I have been mentoring for eight years throughout his graduate school endeavors. He applied at a Midwest university and listed two other professors besides myself as an academic reference. Through the grapevine, he found out one of these former professors did not give him a sterling reference and this possibly could have been the reason why he wasn't offered the job. When he complained to me about this injustice, I asked directly if he asked specifically to the person listed as a reference what they would say if called by the potential employer? He said he didn't think to ask because he just assumed if you give someone permission to list them as a reference, it meant that the response would always be a positive one. Well, you are now finding out that isn't always the case and it's important and yet uncomfortable to ask your potential references what to expect from them. If the reference source states that their potential comments provided wouldn't totally be positive, you should thank them for their sincerity and move on to another legitimate reference source that can provide the information that will support your academic work and your efforts. I have always asked for a physical letter from my references first, supported by a phone call later. It helps with the concept of consistency, meaning it becomes very difficult for a reference to write a positive letter about your abilities and then turn around and contradict this via a phone call to potential employers who have already received this letter. This helps in keeping your references honest and supportive of your efforts, as you pursue the career path.

Most companies or reference checks ask for three to five people to contact so you want to make sure your reference contacts are all in agreement to be that reference check and you have an idea of what will be said of your character or work ethic if they are contacted on your behalf. Also from a personal perspective, it certainly doesn't hurt to send your references a monetary gift card or thank you note for the time they spent speaking about you via a phone call or writing a letter. Letters of support take time to construct and it makes my life a bit more pleasurable when I do get a gift card or a personalized thank you note in the mail. A $5 Starbuck's card isn't much but it goes a long way with the people who are going to perform this duty every time you apply for a position. Just one reference could potentially write five to eight letters to different companies on your behalf. Don't you think that kind of effort should be rewarded, regardless if you got the job? Don't even think about that one since the answer is always "yes." Take care of those who will be taking care of you.

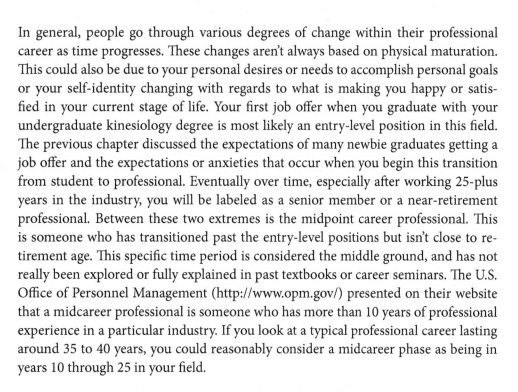

CHAPTER 11
Maintaining the Excitement During Midcareer

In general, people go through various degrees of change within their professional career as time progresses. These changes aren't always based on physical maturation. This could also be due to your personal desires or needs to accomplish personal goals or your self-identity changing with regards to what is making you happy or satisfied in your current stage of life. Your first job offer when you graduate with your undergraduate kinesiology degree is most likely an entry-level position in this field. The previous chapter discussed the expectations of many newbie graduates getting a job offer and the expectations or anxieties that occur when you begin this transition from student to professional. Eventually over time, especially after working 25-plus years in the industry, you will be labeled as a senior member or a near-retirement professional. Between these two extremes is the midpoint career professional. This is someone who has transitioned past the entry-level positions but isn't close to retirement age. This specific time period is considered the middle ground, and has not really been explored or fully explained in past textbooks or career seminars. The U.S. Office of Personnel Management (http://www.opm.gov/) presented on their website that a midcareer professional is someone who has more than 10 years of professional experience in a particular industry. If you look at a typical professional career lasting around 35 to 40 years, you could reasonably consider a midcareer phase as being in years 10 through 25 in your field.

Every midcareer opportunist has chosen a path to follow based on personal and professional needs. However, some commonalities do develop with this stage of one's career that weren't a consideration during their first several years as a working professional. At this stage of one's life, a major difference between an entry-level professional and a midcareer opportunist is the expertise you have developed in a particular area in the field. The position that you possess is no longer an entry or beginning career level stepping stone. Midcareer kinesiology professionals are usually seeking additional opportunities, thinking about new career alternatives. Many at this stage of their lives have families of their own and look for work-life balance within their professional life. This is a crossroad at this important stage of your life where midcareer professionals either become more passionate about their occupation or become burned out by the predictability of their mundane job.

Based on my own past experiences, I was very fortunate to find mentors and forecast the possibilities of what and how my career would play out. I wasn't told of a "mid-career opportunity" or explained about job burnout by anyone, but I saw this in co-workers, which served to remind myself of important choices to make based on your own professional and personal goals set early on in this process. As I mentioned in an earlier chapter, when I first entered the workforce as an entry-level professional in corporate fitness, I was clueless about industry patterns for employment retention and its hierarchy. I was very fortunate to be employed in a financial institution where the people I was personal training would discuss the politics and realities of the corporate shark tank. It was uplifting to me to hear of stories of hostile takeovers in the financial industry and why there was no such thing as job security in banking. This provided enough insight to know that I most likely would not be working for this employer over the next 25 years. I was a small fish in a large aquarium and in order to move up in the hierarchy chain, I had to be proactive and more observant towards the changes in the kinesiology industry. My work hours allowed the best approach to improving my career opportunities to qualify for and attend graduate school in the evenings. Did I know at that time what a master's degree would do for my career? Of course not but I knew somehow if I stayed stagnant, I wouldn't be in any position to sell myself at the next level so going back to school and hoping additional education and opportunities would arise was the goal over the next two years while maintaining my position as an exercise specialist with the First Interstate Bancorp.

During my first year of graduate school, several classmates and I would walk by the job board located near the Career Center building at the university. We would just casually look to see what was posted and sometimes a relevant job would appear that would catch our attention. I had a full-time job already and wasn't looking to find another full-time job, especially since I enjoyed what I did and the convenience of the hours and location. One day, a classmate pointed out a listing for a part-time evening fitness lab instructor at a local community college. I remembered he turned to me and said I would be a good candidate for this position and to apply for it. I was a bit surprised since I did not have interest as an undergraduate towards teaching K-12. So why would I have interest teaching at the community college level? After reading the posting again, I realized I did qualify for the position based on my exercise science background, was pursuing my master's degree, and the hours offered would work with my registered courses I was taking at the time.

I ended up interviewing for the part-time position the next day. The community college was located in the inner city and had a reputation for being a tough place to work based on the type of inner-city students who attended the institution. My first impression wasn't the best since my experiences of being at community colleges were the ones in the suburbs with well-maintained landscaping. This place was in the middle of a busy industrial section of the city with no architectural appeal. As I took 10 steps past my car towards the wrought iron fence that surrounded the buildings, my first thought was to turn around and head back to my car since this was a big mistake. Somehow, a voice inside me said, "You drove here so you might as well complete the interview." I met the department chair of physical education, an older man of Italian descent named Mr. Courtney Borio. After discussing my background, he showed me around and the facility wasn't what I expected. It looked like something you would see in old movies from the 1950s. He said he was looking for someone who could modernize the curriculum and bring in fresh ideas to an evening course that community members and students would take to fulfill their general education requirement towards their associate's degree. There was something about his voice and look that reassured me that this would be an exciting challenge to take on and something inside of me was encouraging to take the part-time job and he was right. This new experience of teaching adults about fitness was much different than I had envisioned and from Day 1, I knew I was making a difference with these students by their body language and comments. I continued with my corporate fitness day job, went to my graduate classes twice a week, and taught an evening fitness lab course during my off days from class. During one of my evening fitness labs, Mr. Borio came in to perform a teaching observation and afterwards, pulled me aside and said it was one of the best-run classes he had seen in a long time. He then asked how long it would be before I graduated with my master's degree. I said I was hopefully completing this soon and asked why? He said a full-time opening in his department would be advertised soon and if I played my cards right, I could have the position starting the following academic year and he was right. I did earn the job and decided to leave the corporate fitness industry and head into my next journey in higher education.

As mentioned earlier in this chapter, midcareer changes usually take place within seven to ten years in the same type industry. But there are times when a change in career happens earlier. It's in a different direction due to either chance or a change in goals you have designed based on information you have been given that propels you to switch your career direction. In my case, I was given information that allowed me to realize that my corporate fitness position would hold uncertainty based on the rocky environment in the financial industry. I was fortunate to be proactive and prepare for changing careers when I did. Two years later, the First Interstate Bancorp was sold to Wells Fargo. The new owners did not retain the First Interstate Bancorp corporate fitness staff and everyone was laid off within six months of the buyout. Wells Fargo ended up bringing in their own corporate wellness staff to take over the facility and I was thankful I was able to secure a great position in a different industry or I would have been in a vulnerable position. I hope you, the reader, will prepare for such change during your career path journey.

Characteristics of a Midcareer Professional

When is it decided that you are no longer an entry-level professional? Is it when someone in your field tells you this or do you receive a telegram in the mail announcing this transformation? Well, it's neither of these. Earlier in the chapter, it was announced through another organization that surviving 10 years would be a good sign. I believe it is more than just longevity in the same field of study. It is when you have identified the following issues as becoming priorities in your life:

1. Obtaining or modifying changes in term life insurance
2. Scrutinizing your annual or quarterly statements for your pension or 401K benefits
3. Quality of time at home increases compared to the amount of time spent at work
4. Medical appointments are more frequent than before
5. Wardrobe change presents an understanding of who you are
6. Your taste in movies or television shows reflects your maturity
7. Passing judgment on newbie hires as entry-level professionals
8. Complaints of how certain goods or services aren't as good as in years past
9. Waiting in line or for services rendered becomes a virtue
10. Attempting to define yourself as different than your parents were at this stage in their lives

As you progress through the stages of professional existence, your desired culture and values evolve. Midcareer professionals often want diversity in their work and in the people they work with. After proving themselves early in their careers, they also commonly want recognition for accomplishments. Experienced midcareer professionals often focus more on the cultural values of the organization, along with the work itself. Family-friendly, flexible, and positive workplaces are often preferred.

Making the Transition

Ambitious people constantly look for new career opportunities, more challenging environments, and new responsibilities. Many midcareer professionals eventually want management or leadership roles. Those with stronger ambitions may even seek progression to upper management and look for advice through their sage mentors who are still active in the field. As you near the second half of a professional career, it is common to look for greater stability, additional insurance benefits, and other advantages that come from having developed a reputation as a seasoned and accomplished veteran in kinesiology.

Is the mid-professional stage related to a mid-life crisis?

We earlier defined a mid-professional career phase but could this be related to experiencing a mid-life crisis? A mid-life crisis is a concept of uncertainty within yourself based on either emotions or events that spark the question if you are happy or accepting at this stage in your life. People who are questioning if they are at happy at a stage in their career could experience the following characteristics:

- An obsession with exercise routines and improving their physical appearance
- Depression due to their inability to be satisfied at work
- Boredom with activities that were considered fun
- Feeling a need for adventure and excitement
- Questioning the choices and decisions about their job
- Confusion about where they are in their life
- Anger at others who they feel have blocked their career goals
- A sense of remorse for not completing certain goals
- Acting on emotions to seek a higher risk or choosing a different career path
- A desire to achieve a feeling when they were in their 20s

Most often a mid-life crisis is defined well into the process of change at a certain mid-age. This is because it becomes most visible after a drastic shift in one's career. However, the physical changes have already started long before you see the obvious characteristics as listed above. It's possible to make several adjustments to your life to fit what will make you more content and happy. Being proactive and listening to your thoughts and emotions during this stage can assist with bypassing and continuing with being satisfied with your current job and leading towards more life satisfaction when you approach this milestone.

Preventing the Symptoms of Mid-Life Crisis That Affect Your Mid-Professional Status

Experiencing a mid-life crisis only affects those professionals who are not setting goals constantly as described in this text as well as reflecting on a regular basis of determining if you are happy with your career status. If you happen to miss the boat during the last several years and happen to hit this critical stage, this isn't something you make an appointment with a doctor and seek a treatment for. This represents a time of awakening when a person is looking for a change to expand their life and create the change to promote a happy career, leading towards a healthy retirement from this field. Instead of discussing what can be done about shifting to better fit when the giant hole has already been dug, the topic for you as a student is to have a full understanding to what not to do. Developing a mid-life crisis based on your mid-professional career status is a biological and psychological process due to changes that occur when you get older. One way to help recognize and prevent this from happening to you is to take a slight step backwards in order to move forward. Moving in this direction allows you to learn new skills since method is a great example of obtaining additional education. I remind myself of a lecture I had in an undergraduate biology course. All species have to evolve within their life or die. The best resolution to preventing a mid-life crisis within your kinesiology profession is learning to embrace the fact that changes must eventually occur throughout one's life and to stay competitive, your methods must be transformative within your career field. To do nothing is to let this disease in and you will eventually pass away based on the rules of evolution. A crisis still invokes a change of behavior but it's a change towards the worst career and life scenario that a person no longer can control and often negatively affects everyone you either work or live with. This would not be the method to pursue.

Another concern is the influence of the current Western lifestyle where happiness or success is based upon amount of dollars you earn and not the goals you achieved. Many people are so focused on their monthly or annual incomes they forget to embrace what true success is all about. Sadly, this pursuit of happiness allows a faster path of hitting the mid-life crisis through your unhappy job status and outlook. Instead of looking at the problem in terms of money made or invested only, focus on your contributions to humanity and what you can do to make your family and dependents proud of what you represent in this global environment.

What can I infuse passion and excitement back into my kinesiology career?

Here are my personal tips to infuse this passion and use your experience from your undergraduate studies to promote overall happiness and the pursuit towards finding virtue.

1. Leave each job or position in a better place than when you arrive.
2. Even if your position or status involved conflict, do not burn a bridge when transitioning to the next job or career.
3. Allow time on a daily basis to self-reflect on how you are performing or taking necessary steps to achieve your next goal.
4. Keep in touch with those professors or advisors who you connected with at least once a year.
5. Always update your resume or CV every few months to remind yourself of your next career step.
6. Maintain a stress reduction routine, may this be an exercise routine or another form of therapy.
7. Take time to build other interests within your kinesiology work. This could pay off someday.
8. Even though it costs money, maintain professional memberships and travel to a professional conference at least once a year to meet new professionals in your field.

9. Whenever you have a chance encounter that provides you with assistance, send a thank you card or an email acknowledging this helpful act or thought.

10. Develop and maintain relationships with positive and ambitious people. This tends to rub off on others and keeps your disappointments very diminutive vs. your overall successes.

L A B
Introduction of Kinesiology Faculty

NAME_____ DATE:_____

Directions

Locate the following faculty members and physically introduce yourself. Once you have established this contact, please have them sign off on this sheet. Fill in the rest of the information before submitting this for full credit consideration to your professor.

Instructor/Professor: _____

Specialty or research interests: _____

Instructor/Professor:_____

Specialty or research interests: _____

Instructor/Professor:_____

Specialty or research interests: _____

Instructor/Professor:_____

Specialty or research interests: _____

Instructor/Professor:_____

Specialty or research interests: _____

Instructor/Professor:_____

Specialty or research interests: _____

Instructor/Professor:_____

Specialty or research interests: _____

LAB
Learning Strategies Lab

NAME _____ DATE: _____

Taking Stock of Your Learning Strategies

We take seriously the importance of your ability to develop your self-reflection skills in this course. Throughout this lab manual, you will find self-assessments like this one to help you develop insights into your own behavior.

In this first exercise, review the elements of effective learning and, for each of them, indicate whether you think it is an area of strength you already demonstrate in your approach to new courses or if it may be an area in which you could use some improvement.

Strength	*Could be improved*	
_____	_____	I manage my time effectively to complete course assignments.
_____	_____	I use study environments that reduce distractions.
_____	_____	I can concentrate on my studies without losing too much time to daydreaming.
_____	_____	I read my text carefully to capture critical concepts and ideas.
_____	_____	I listen carefully and make meaningful notes during lecture and classroom activities.
_____	_____	I organize and reorganize ideas to help me grasp main points and key concepts rather than memorize everything I read or hear.
_____	_____	I rehearse materials until they are "over-learned" to enhance my effectiveness on objective tests.
_____	_____	I devote a sufficient amount of time using properly spaced study sessions in order to avoid last-minute cramming for tests.
_____	_____	I involve myself personally by looking for how the ideas presented in class connect with and apply to my personal life.
_____	_____	I ask questions about the ideas that are confusing or seem inaccurate or incomplete to me.
_____	_____	I actively evaluate how successful my approach is to the course, based on feedback from my instructor, and make corrections to improve my effectiveness.

Source: Psychology Contexts & Applications, Halonen/Santrock, 3rd ed. (1999)

L A B
Time Management Lab

NAME _____ DATE: _____

Time Start	End	Time Used	Activity-Description

Source: Psychology Contexts & Applications, Halonen/Santrock, 3rd ed. (1999)

L A B
Careers Self-Assessment

NAME _____ DATE: _____

Instructions

The occupations listed below are the fastest growing in the United States. They are arranged by education level. The first column has occupations that are growing at the fastest rate of increase. The second column has occupations that are growing the fastest numerically. Place a check next to any occupations that interest you, then evaluate how seriously you might be considering a career in these fast-growing areas.

	Occupations growing at the fastest (percentage) rates			Occupations having the biggest increases in total number of jobs
	First-professional degree			
☐	Chiropractors		☐	Lawyers
☐	Lawyers		☐	Physicians
☐	Physicians		☐	Clergy
☐	Clergy		☐	Chiropractors
☐	Podiatrists		☐	Dentists
	Doctoral degree			
☐	Medical scientists		☐	College and university faculty
☐	Biological scientists		☐	Biological scientists
☐	College and university faculty		☐	Medical scientists
☐	Mathematicians and all other mathematical scientists		☐	Mathematicians and all other mathematical scientists
	Master's degree			
☐	Operations research analysts		☐	Management analysts
☐	Speech-language pathologists and audiologists		☐	Counselors
☐	Management analysts		☐	Speech-language pathologists and audiologists
☐	Counselors		☐	Psychologists
☐	Urban and regional planners		☐	Operations research analysts

Work experience plus bachelor's degree			
☐	Engineering, mathematics, and natural science managers	☐	General managers and top executives
☐	Marketing, advertising, and public relations managers	☐	Fitness managers
☐	Artists and commercial artists	☐	Marketing, advertising, and public relations managers
☐	Financial managers	☐	Engineering, mathematics, and natural science managers
☐	Athletic administrators	☐	Education administrators
Bachelor's degree			
☐	Marketing analysts	☐	Marketing analysts
☐	Medical sales	☐	Teachers, secondary school
☐	Occupational therapists	☐	Teachers, elementary school
☐	Physical therapists	☐	Teachers, special education
☐	Sport facility management	☐	Exercise specialists
Associate degree			
☐	Paralegals	☐	Registered nurses
☐	Medical records technicians	☐	Paralegals
☐	Dental hygienists	☐	Personal trainers
☐	Respiratory therapists	☐	Dental hygienists
☐	Physical therapy assistants	☐	Medical records technicians

Source: Occupational Outlook Handbook, table 1, p. 7. (1996-1997)

L A B
Networking/Getting to Know Your Classmates Lab

NAME _____ DATE: _____

Drives a red car	Owns a fur coat	Likes 80's music	Mom is a homemaker	Dad served in the military
Is an only child	Has a pet dog	Played high school baseball	Went to a private high school	Has eaten at In and Out Burger
Has traveled to a foreign country	Has taken a ballet class before	Has been to North Dakota	Knows how to drive a 5-speed stick shift	Worked at a fast-food restaurant
Favorite color is purple	Has a tattoo	Broke their arm	Went to a charter high school	Has more than 4 siblings
Knows how to juggle 3 tennis balls	Has never eaten sushi	Watches *American Idol* regularly	Favorite football team is the Dallas Cowboys	This female can do more than 5 chinups
Can wiggle their ears	Speaks another language fluently	Family owns a farm	Family has a record player at home	Knows who Jack LaLanne is
Knows how to ride a motorcycle	Won an official contest in their past	Wore braces in junior high/middle school	Been to Disneyland	Has never visited Mt. Rushmore

Directions:

Write the name of your classmate who matches the characteristic listed in each box. Once you have completed this, submit it to your instructor. Any unnamed boxes will lead to incomplete points tabulation. All names must be legible for full credit.

L A B
Career Presentation Lab Information and Grading Rubric

NAME_____ DATE: _____

Directions: During and near the end of our readings from the textbook, *Exploring the Field of Kinesiology in the Twenty-First Century*, the student should be thinking about the type of career in the field of kinesiology to pursue.

Based on this concept, the 50-point presentation will be based upon interviewing a person who is currently performing this profession (not family related) and providing a verbal PowerPoint presentation that will cover the following criteria:

1. Introduction of yourself and your personal and academic background (5 points)
2. Introduction of the interviewee and why you selected this person and the specific profession (5 points)
3. Their background and how and why they ended up in this specific profession (20 points)
4. Words of advice to anyone pursuing this specific occupation in KSS (5 points)
5. How this ties in or relates to your textbook readings (5 points)
6. What you did and did not know regarding the steps to obtain in order to qualify for this occupation (5 points)
7. Adding anything extra or visual that improves the presentation to the audience (5 points)
8. Presentation must be longer than 5 minutes but not exceed 10 minutes.

Introduction – informative and clear	5 points max./ 3 points, vague/1 point, not clear
Clear rationale of interviewee selection/profession	5 points max./3 points, vague/1 point, not clear
Career steps are clear and 10 questions are pertinent	20 points max./15 point, questions not clear or pertinent/10 points, missing information/Less than 10 points, incomplete
Understanding on how to improve chances of success	5 points max./ 5 points, vague/1 point, not clear
Information ties or does not tie into the text	5 points max/3 points, did not cite references in text/1 point, no citation
Information added to base of knowledge	5 points max/3 points, vague/1 point, not clear
Anything extra to the presentation to improve audience participation or attention	5 point max/3 points, vague/1 point, not included
Total points:	50 points max

L A B
Sample Resume

NAME _____ DATE: _____

Directions: Use the following sample to put together your resume. Submit this to your instructor for credit when completed. The resume should be only 1 page.

John Doe
3305 Elm Street, Apt. #25
Great Falls, SD, 57069
(605) 999-9999
John.doe@westsd.edu
http://www.physicalfitnet.com/sample

Career Objective:
Have the ability to use my skills to promote health and wellness to a corporate fitness program.

Education:

The University of West Dakota: Great Falls, SD
Undergraduate degree: Kinesiology – Exercise Science Specialization
Expected Graduation: December 2016

Professional Experience:

- Division I College Swimming Participant (2014)
- City of Lincoln Parks and Recreation Volunteer (2012)
- 2012 West Dakota State NSCA Conference Participant

Work Experience:

- **Kinesiology & Sport Science Student Volunteer**   Great Falls, SD
  Administrative duties as needed   May 2011- August 2012

- **City of Lincoln Parks and Recreation**   Lincoln, NE
  Lifeguard   Summers 2003 – 2009

Certifications:

AFAA Personal Fitness Trainer   July 2013
CPR, First Aid, AED   May 2013
Certified Lifeguard   May 2012

References provided upon request